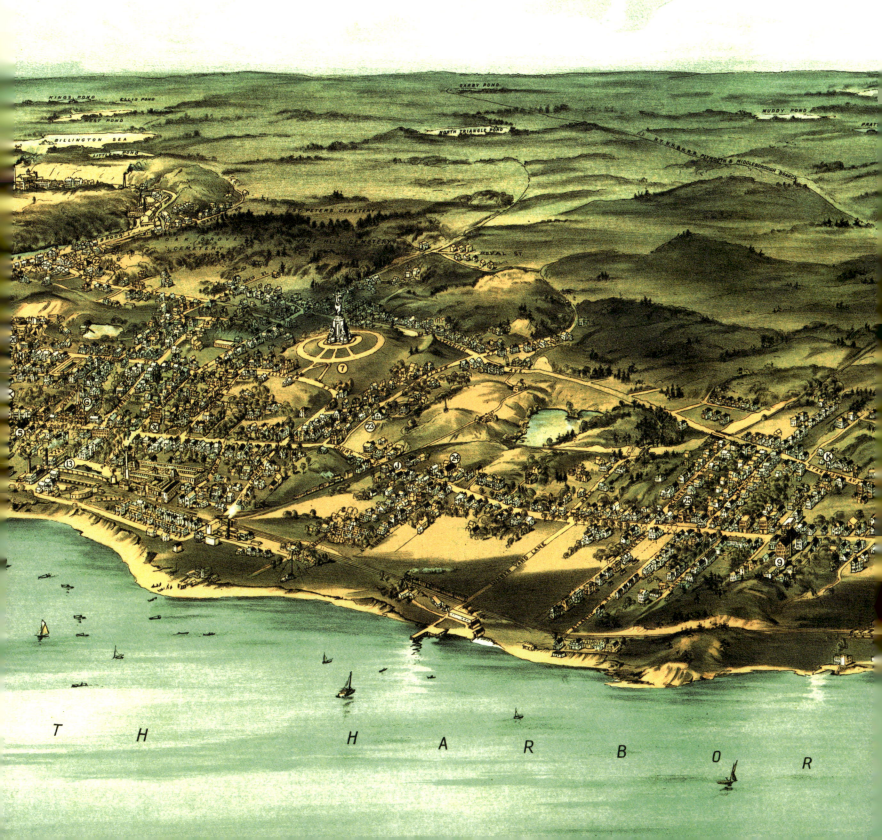

FOREFATHERS MONUMENT GUIDEBOOK

Copyright ©2021 by Michelle Gallagher

All rights reserved. No part of this book may be reproduced in any manner without written permission from the publisher, except in the case of brief quotations in articles and reviews with proper attribution.

Published by Proclamation Press, a division of Proclamation House, Inc.

Printed in the United States of America.

Library of Congress Control Number: 2022912039

ISBN 978-1-7379016-2-4

Cover image provided by Hawk Visuals, Plymouth, Massachusetts

Except where noted, interior photography provided by Sojourner Media, Plymouth, Massachusetts

Layout and Design by Michelle Gallagher

For sales or media inquiries, contact:

PROCLAMATION HOUSE, INC.

6 Main Street Ext #3554, Plymouth, MA 02361
www.ProclamationHouse.org
Tel: (774) 766-7122
info@proclamationhouse.org

FOREFATHERS MONUMENT
GUIDEBOOK

• HOW THE PILGRIMS ESTABLISHED SELF-GOVERNMENT AT PLYMOUTH COLONY •

Michelle Gallagher

INTRODUCTION

I first became aware of the Forefathers Monument when our family moved to a home near the Plymouth waterfront. Walking our dog in the new neighborhood one evening, my husband and I climbed a hill on Allerton Street and noticed a statue peeking out from behind the trees. *What on earth is that?* Moving closer, we saw the enormous statue of a woman with several figures seated below her in the middle of a large circular pathway. The location was puzzling. *Who did this? How did it get here?*

Walking our dog to the monument soon became part of our weekly routine, and with each visit, my curiosity grew. I love traveling, and whenever I visit someplace new, I like to check the gift shop for a guidebook as a souvenir of my trip. *Shouldn't an impressive monument like this have a guidebook to explain it?* To hear my husband's side of the story, I talked about it long enough that he finally told me to do something about it. This book is the result of his good-natured prodding, and while this project grew into far more than either of us imagined—I am deeply grateful for his support and encouragement as we set off on this adventure together.

A few items of note. First, this guidebook was designed so readers could dip in and out of the material according to their interests. For those who read it more traditionally, from start to finish, I hope that any overlapping areas of storytelling only enhance your appreciation of the Pilgrim story. Also, because I rely on many historical sources such as William Bradford's journal—terms such as *Natives, Native Indian,* or *Indian* are used throughout this book. To preserve historical accuracy, I have included these outdated terms in their original context. In no way is this meant to disparage indigenous people, who today are more appropriately identified by individual tribes, or referred to as *Native Americans, Indian Americans,* or *First Nations People*. Their presence and contributions are integral to the Pilgrim story, and I hope this project also honors them.

This guidebook is divided into two sections. The first section covers the physical history of the monument—its conception, design, funding, and relevance over the years. But to appreciate *why* the Forefathers Monument was built, it's essential to understand what motivated a generation of citizens to erect it in the first place—so we begin with the story of the Pilgrims. Section two explores the rich symbolism of the monument through the lives of the people who inspired it. Why do *Faith, Morality, Law, Education,* and *Liberty* represent the historical legacy of the Pilgrims? How did these five components create the foundation for self-government at Plymouth Colony? As the Pilgrim's spiritual leader, Pastor John Robinson, wrote: "There is no creature so perfect in wisdom and knowledge but may learn something for time present and to come by times past." Every generation is called to learn from the past to improve the future—and there is much we can learn from the Pilgrims.

President Ronald Reagan once observed: "You and I have within ourselves the God-given right and the ability to determine our own destiny. But freedom is never more than one generation away from extinction. We didn't pass it on to our children in the bloodstream. The only way they can inherit the freedom we have known is if we fight for it—protect it, defend it and then hand it to them—with the well-taught lessons of how they in their lifetime must do the same." In the Pilgrim story, we find the remarkable origins of self-government in America. Their courage, tenacity, and willingness to risk everything in pursuit of faith and freedom are humbling and inspirational. These people were extraordinary, and I hope this book offers a compelling explanation of why the Forefathers Monument was erected "by a grateful people in remembrance of their labors, sacrifices, and sufferings for the cause of civil and religious liberty."

To faith and freedom,

Michelle Gallagher

"This is what the Lord says: 'Stand at the crossroads and look; ask for the ancient paths, ask where the good way is, and walk in it, and you will find rest for your souls.'"

- Jeremiah 6:16

SECTION ONE: HISTORY

The Pilgrims: Setting the Stage for a Rebellion 12
The Pilgrim Society 23
The Architect: Hammatt Billings 24
The Design 26
The Granite 32
The Dedication Ceremony 36
The Monument Throughout History 38
Maintenance and Repairs 40
Interpreting the Monument 42
What Is Hidden Under the Monument? 44

SECTION TWO: SYMBOLISM

FAITH 51
MORALITY 65
  Evangelist 68
  Prophet 70
LAW 77
  Mercy 88
  Justice 90
EDUCATION 97
  Wisdom 106
  Youth 109
LIBERTY 117
  Peace 131
  Tyranny 133

TOPICS:
The History of Plymouth Rock 58
Survivors of the Mayflower 74
Plymouth Colony's Common House: Lot #1 85
The Influence of Women at Plymouth Colony 100
Plymouth & Jamestown: A Tale of Two Colonies 123

PANELS:
Dedication (East Panel) 47
National Registry of Historic Places (East Panel) 47
List of Mayflower Passengers (North & South Panels) 73
Governor Bradford's Quote (West Panel) 95
The Embarkation (Below Morality) 72
Treaty with Massasoit (Below Law) 92
Signing of the Mayflower Compact (Below Education) 112
The Pilgrim's Landing (Below Liberty) 134

APPENDIX:
Footnotes & Endnotes 138
Photography Credits 141
Bibliography 142

FOREFATHERS MONUMENT GUIDEBOOK

SECTION ONE:
HISTORY

"Oh, there have been revolutions before and since ours. But those revolutions simply exchanged one set of rules for another. Ours was a revolution that changed the very concept of government."

- Ronald Reagan (1911-2004), former governor and 40th President of the United States

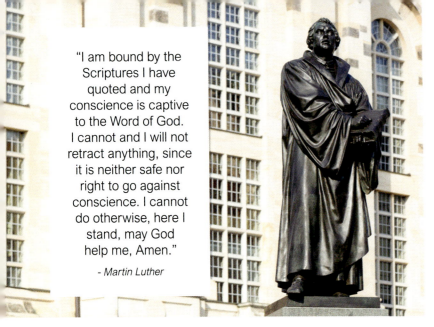

> "I am bound by the Scriptures I have quoted and my conscience is captive to the Word of God. I cannot and I will not retract anything, since it is neither safe nor right to go against conscience. I cannot do otherwise, here I stand, may God help me, Amen."
>
> - Martin Luther

ABOVE: *A statue of Martin Luther in front of the church Frauenkirche in Dresden, Germany.*

SETTING THE STAGE FOR A REBELLION

In the early 16th century, a spiritual revolution was brewing in Europe. In 1517, a German priest by the name of Martin Luther launched a campaign against the Roman Catholic Church—urging a return to Scripture as the sole authority for worship. Luther railed against the church's practice of selling "indulgences" to parishioners to absolve them of their sins, declaring that salvation could never be found in works—but only by faith in Christ alone. This movement became known as the Protestant Reformation, and it would change the course of Western church history. Although Luther was shunned for his ideas and excommunicated from the church, the Reformation movement continued to sweep across Europe, bringing "spiritual revival as well as dramatic political change."[1]

A decade later in 1527, England's King Henry VIII launched his own fiery campaign against the Roman Catholic Church—but for far different reasons. After his marriage to Catherine of Aragon failed to produce an heir, King Henry petitioned the church for an annulment. Henry was infatuated with one of his wife's ladies-in-waiting and wanted out of his marriage to Catherine to marry his paramour, Anne Boleyn. When the Pope denied his request for an annulment, Henry was outraged. Breaking all ties with the Catholic Church, he then established the Church of England, also called the Anglican church, and assumed the official title of *Supreme Head*. In 1534, England's *Act of Supremacy* confirmed Henry's supremacy over the church, requiring all nobility to swear an oath to the same. Now the absolute ruler of his kingdom, King Henry was no longer subject to the Pope's authority.

In a shrewd move to consolidate power, Henry perpetrated one of the biggest land grabs in history. Confiscating all existing monasteries, the vast property holdings of the Catholic church were immediately annexed by the crown. In one huge takeover, Henry amassed an astonishing amount of wealth. Many of these property acquisitions were subsequently awarded to his followers as gifts to reward their continuing support. Even though Henry's split with the Catholic church was self-serving, "many people in England were ready for a change, seized the opportunity, and embraced the Reformation. After years of attempting to suppress the printing of the Bible

BELOW: *"Portrait of Henry VIII" by painter Hans Holbein the Younger.*

Fidei Defensor — "Defender of the Faith"

In 1517, Martin Luther sent shockwaves across Europe when he wrote his "Ninety-Five Theses" to protest the corruption of the Catholic Church. In response, King Henry VIII wrote a public defense of the church and dedicated it to the Pope—an act of loyalty which earned Henry the lofty title, *Fidei Defensor*, or *"Defender of the Faith."* In a twist of irony, Henry would later abandon the Catholic Church to establish the Church of England.

ABOVE: *Known as "Bloody Mary" for her deadly persecution of Protestants across England, Queen Mary ruthlessly ordered the execution of her own cousin Lady Jane, as depicted below.*

in English, King Henry begrudgingly reversed course, and officially sanctioned an English language Bible."[2] In doing so, he unwittingly sparked the embers of a spiritual revival in England.

When King Henry died in 1547, the deep rivalry between the Protestants and Catholics only intensified as each of his children rose to power. The Reformation movement thrived under Henry's young son, Edward VI—but when Edward died just six years later, he was succeeded by his half-sister Mary. A devout Catholic, Queen Mary did everything in her power to cleanse the church of Protestants. Mary's first order as Queen was to execute Lady Jane Grey, her Protestant cousin, and competition to the throne. Mary would order over 300 religious dissenters to be burned at the stake, a violent spree that earned her the title, "Bloody Mary." Her reign lasted for five years until 1558 when Mary died after a prolonged illness.

ABOVE: *After the death of Queen Mary, Elizabeth I was the next in line to succeed her half-sister to the throne in 1559.*

After the death of Queen Mary, the monarchy passed to her half-sister Elizabeth, who was herself a committed Protestant. To placate the warring factions of Catholics and Protestants within the church, the newly crowned Queen proposed the *Elizabethan Religious Settlement*. "It was a compromise of sorts: the Church of England would retain its Protestant doctrine, but it would also keep familiar, Catholic-style worship ceremonies and traditions. The publication of English language Bibles, once outlawed in England, now proliferated, and commoners and gentry alike eagerly purchased personal copies. Learning and sharing Scripture became the rage in England."[3] Just as her father before her, Queen Elizabeth had unwittingly fanned the flames of a spiritual revival in England.

"Nine Days Queen" *Lady Jane Gray*

When young King Edward VI became deathly ill, his advisors worked persuasively to convince him to modify the rights of succession to ensure that a Protestant inherited the throne. Before he died, Edward altered the order of succession to skip his Catholic half-sister Mary in favor of his Protestant cousin—Lady Jane Grey. Jane was crowned in a private ceremony, but her reign was famously short-lived. After hearing of Jane's coronation, Mary and her advisors claimed it was unlawful—arguing that Edward was manipulated on his deathbed. Several days later, in a cunning display of political theater, Mary and her supporters marched into London in a huge display of public support. Soon after that, Lady Jane Grey was arrested for high treason and England's "Nine Days Queen" was publicly beheaded.

LEFT: *"The Execution of Lady Jane Grey" is depicted by French artist Paul Delaroche in his 1833 work.*

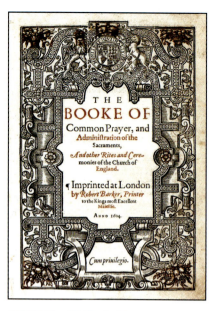

ABOVE: *The 1604 Book of Common Prayer.*

THE PILGRIMS EMERGE

The Pilgrims came of age during this time when the institutions of church and government were inexorably linked. By 1558, England's *Act of Uniformity* required every citizen to attend church services regardless of their personal beliefs—or face a stiff penalty. The *Book of Common Prayer* was the only approved form of church liturgy, and any worship services conducted apart from it were illegal. Those who disobeyed the church's rules were labeled "non-conformist" and considered a traitor to the crown. Acts of religious "heresy" were swiftly prosecuted, and some offenses were even punishable by death.

By the late 16th century, the proliferation of Bibles and increase in personal Bible study had led to divisions in the church. One group known as *Puritans* had emerged, so named for their desire to "purify" or purge the church of any beliefs or practices that were not rooted in Scripture. "Queen Elizabeth's compromise of Protestant doctrine and Catholic-style ceremony was generally acceptable to much of the English population, but it deeply troubled England's Puritans," who believed that the church's ornate ceremonies had shifted the true focus of worship from God to man.[4] "They resisted the Church of England requirement to bow at the church altar, which they viewed as misplaced devotion. They were offended by liturgical ceremonies, which they saw as man-centered and prideful… and detracted from humble, Bible-based worship."[5]

ABOVE: *A view of the ornate interior of Winchester Cathedral in England.*

> *A Parte of a Register* and *Seconde Parte of a Register,* issued in the reign of Elizabeth, pointed out the distressing fact that there were many incompetent clergy in the parishes.
>
> "Lewd," "of scandalous life," "a drunkard," "a grievous swearer," "a bad liver," "a gamester," "his conversation is mostly in hounds," "a very careless person, he had a childe by a maid since he was instituted and inducted"— these were some of the descriptions of the clergy at the time.
>
> Source: *The Faith of the Pilgrims* by Robert Bartlett

ABOVE: *Originally founded in 642, Winchester Cathedral was seized by King Henry VIII when he broke with the Catholic Church.*

Those who identified themselves as Puritans believed that many of the church's rules and practices violated clear Biblical instructions. They believed that Christ Himself—*not the monarch*—was the true head of God's Church. Puritans also disagreed with the controlling arm of the church hierarchy. Clergy appointments were often handed out as political rewards, and many of the local parishes were suffering under the leadership of ill-suited, even immoral clergymen. Scandals were increasingly common. However, the Puritans continued advocating for reforms from inside the church. "Despite their call for reforms, mainstream Puritans were still officially members of the Church of England, and in most cases their protests were not considered to be treasonous."[6]

SEPARATISTS DEFY THE CHURCH

At the same time, a smaller, more radical sect within the larger Puritan movement held a far more dangerous view. Called *Separatists* for their desire to leave or "separate" from the Church of England, this group believed the entire institution was corrupt beyond any repair. "Separatists felt called by Scripture and conscience to worship outside the authority of the Church of England, and in their day that was a criminal act under English law."[7] For Separatists, the man-made rules and rituals of Anglican church worship had become too much to bear. Choosing to leave rather than compromise the principles of their faith, Separatists went underground to worship in so-called "separating" churches across England—an act of treason. By following their conscience and leaving the Anglican church, Separatists instantly became fugitives from the law.

ABOVE: *William Brewster of Scrooby, and a young William Bradford of Austerfield were both regular attendees of Richard Clifton's services at All Saints' Church. Today, the same footpath these men used to walk from their homes to the church in Babworth is known as "The Pilgrims' Way."*

Taking a stand for their beliefs, these Separatists became the conscientious objectors of their day. *William Bradford. John Carver. Isaac Allerton. William Brewster.* "The men we know as Pilgrims were Separatists—regarded by most decent people in their time as revolutionaries, radicals, a threat to the state. These radicals are the men we now revere as the staid, conservative bed-rock founders of our nation."[8] William Bradford chronicled their reasons for leaving the Anglican church, writing: "They realized not only that these base ceremonies were unlawful, but also that the tyrannous power of the prelates ought not to be submitted to, since it was contrary to the freedom of the gospel and would burden men's consciences and… profane the worship of God."[9]

Many Separatists moved to the countryside to avoid detection by authorities. It was here, in the small English village of Babworth, that many like-minded reformers flocked to hear the sermons of Richard Clifton, the pastor at All Saints' Church. Clifton's captivating preaching style had a deep impact on the early Pilgrims, especially William Brewster, who lived just five miles away in the nearby village of Scrooby. When Clifton was removed from his parish for preaching on reforms, Brewster invited Clifton and his family—now homeless and without means—to come to live in his manor house at Scrooby and preach to a growing number of people who would one day be known as Pilgrims.

LEFT: *All Saints' Church in Babworth, where Richard Clifton preached from 1586 until 1604.*

Brewster's home at Scrooby was a "sprawling, two-story brick-and-timber manor house with almost forty rooms and a chapel," and it quickly became a meeting hub for these early reformers.[10] Scrooby Manor belonged to the Archbishop of York, and William's father had worked as the estate's bailiff for over thirty years. William studied at Cambridge before serving as a diplomatic secretary under Queen Elizabeth. When he returned to Scrooby in 1589 to care for his ailing father, William assumed his father's duties of postmaster and bailiff. As one of Scrooby's more prominent citizens, William Brewster risked his reputation and livelihood by opening his home to these early Pilgrim meetings— joining ranks with religious dissenters who were being actively pursued by the authorities.

Brewster was also familiar with John Robinson, who had recently been stripped of his post at St. Andrews Church in Norwich due to his Separatist leanings. Brewster invited Robinson and his family to join them at Scrooby, and Robinson began to assist Clifton in pastoring the growing congregation. "In 1606 the Scrooby congregation was formed. After consenting to the covenant, the members chose Clyfton as pastor, Robinson as teacher, and Brewster as elder."[11] Years later in his journal, Bradford recounted the vows he took as a young man in Scrooby: "As the Lord's free people joined themselves together by covenant as a church, in the fellowship of the gospel to walk in all His ways, made known, or to be made known to them, according to their best endeavours, whatever it should cost them, the Lord assisting them."[12]

TOP LEFT: *The entrance to the manor grounds at Scrooby in Nottinghamshire.* **ABOVE:** *Today, the only surviving building from Scrooby Manor is the farmhouse, now a private home.*

> Some prominent leaders of the Separatist movement languished in prison for years before they were publicly executed. The government dispatched spies to infiltrate secret church gatherings as a means to entrap those who were meeting illegally.

And cost them it did. Throughout England, Separatists were hunted down and punished for their religious beliefs. Some prominent leaders of the Separatist movement languished in prison for years before they were publicly executed. The government dispatched spies to infiltrate secret church gatherings as a means to entrap those who were meeting illegally. In time, even members of the Scrooby congregation were exposed and brought before the magistrate. "Some were clapped into prison; others had their houses watched night and day, and escaped with difficulty; and most were obliged to fly, and leave their homes and means of livelihood."[13] By 1607, the Scrooby church had reached its breaking point. "Seeing that they could no longer continue under such circumstances, they resolved to get over to Holland as soon as they could," and join other Separatists who had already left England for the more religiously tolerant Netherlands.[14]

ABOVE: *A traditional Delft blue Dutch tile of a sailing vessel.*

A NEW LIFE IN HOLLAND

After several dangerous attempts, the Pilgrims made the journey safely to Holland. They settled in the bustling city of Leiden, where the church blossomed and thrived under the leadership of their pastor, John Robinson. Finally, the congregation who first gathered in Scrooby was free to worship God "according to the simplicity of the gospel and without the mixture of men's inventions, and… be ruled by the laws of God's word… according to the Scriptures." [15] But life in Leiden was a far cry from England's quaint country villages. The Pilgrims struggled to learn the language and customs of a new country. To make ends meet, entire families—children included—worked long, physically grueling hours in Leiden's textile factories. Many of the Pilgrims worked as weavers, cobblers, pipe-makers, bakers, and dock workers in the commercial trades. Although the free expression of their faith was a great comfort, life in Holland was hard. For some, the sacrifices were simply too much to bear. Many who remained in England refused to join the church at Leiden—preferring to "submit to bondage, with danger to their conscience, rather than endure" the hardships of life in the Netherlands. [16]

> "It is difficult for us today to imagine the courage it took for the Saints to decide to leave England. Virtually none of these men and women had ever been more than a few miles from their rural homes. Crossing the North Sea to Amsterdam meant turning their backs on the only world they had ever known, almost certainly never to return. The move to Holland, Bradford wrote: "Was by many thought an adventure almost desperate; a case intolerable and a misery worse than death." Their own fears were not the only barriers that the Saints had to overcome. Since government approval was required for all travel abroad and this was automatically denied to religious dissenters, the Separatists would have to sneak out of the country, like thieves."
>
> Source: *William Bradford* by Kieran Doherty

ABOVE: *A depiction of St. Peters' Church in Leiden, entitled "Pieterskerk of Leiden" by Dutch artist Frederik de Wit. Pieterskerk was the focal point of the cityscape, and where many of the Pilgrims who died in Holland were buried.*

By 1617, the congregation had lived in Leiden for over a decade and certain realities could no longer be ignored. Although they "bore these difficulties very cheerfully, and with resolute courage" as the price of their religious freedom—this strenuous lifestyle had taken a toll on the church. [17] "Old age began to steal on many of them, and their great and continual labours, with other crosses and sorrows, hastened it before their time." [18] Over thirty family members died during the Pilgrim's exile in Holland, and many were buried at *Pieterskerk*—St. Peter's Church—alongside their Leiden neighbors. To amplify these painful losses, the congregation's adults had aged prematurely from years of physically demanding labor, and their children had become demoralized by the endless cycle of work.

Holland's worldly culture posed another set of concerns. The same permissive society that welcomed persecuted refugees—also teemed with immorality and a proclivity for personal decadence. Living in an environment so counter-culture to their own beliefs proved challenging, and many parents struggled to exert a godly influence over their children. Some stood by heartbroken, as their children succumbed to temptation and departed from the faith—and were lost to carnal pursuits.

After years of adapting to the Dutch way of life, the Pilgrims feared they were losing their own unique identity. They agonized over how to preserve their faith and English culture—and successfully pass it down to the next generation. Failing that, every other sacrifice would be in vain.

ABOVE: *In "Beware of Luxury," Dutch painter Jan Steen captured the cultural excesses Holland was known for.*

Holland was also changing politically. The peace treaty with Spain was nearing an end, which brought uncertainty and rumors of war. If Spain prevailed in a war against Holland, the Pilgrims feared it could lead to the same religious persecution they experienced at home in England. It was a deeply unsettling time. To discern God's will for the church, the congregation entered into a time of fasting and prayer—and concluded it was time to leave Holland. After weighing their options, they agreed that America offered the best opportunity for a new start. England's ruling monarch, King James I, had authorized efforts to colonize the North American coast, and there was already a permanent settlement in Jamestown, Virginia. But the Pilgrims also knew that joining the Jamestown colony meant a return to the unbiblical rules of Anglican worship—a move that was unthinkable.

BELOW: *Dutch artist Isaac van Swanenburg portrayed the grueling physical labor of Leiden's textile industry; each oil painting was titled to depict the nature of the work.*

"The Removal of the Wool from the Skins and the Combing"

"Washing the Skins and Grading the Wool"

"Spinning Wool"

ABOVE: *In 1606, King James authorized the British colonization of North America.*

Undeterred, the church considered the idea of planting a colony elsewhere in the Virginia territories, further north of the Jamestown settlement. To proceed, they would need the King's permission, a legal land patent, and money to finance the entire endeavor—all of which seemed impossibly out of reach.

THE VIRGINIA COMPANY

ABOVE: *The official seal of the Virginia Company of London.*

Nevertheless, over the next few years the congregation worked diligently toward these goals. In London, King James authorized a joint-stock venture called the Virginia Company to issue land patents for a huge territory of land along the North American coast. John Carver and Robert Cushman, two deacons in the Leiden church, traveled to England on behalf of the congregation to petition the Virginia Company for a land patent. Through a lengthy process of personal visits and written correspondence, the church sought to dispel concerns from company officials or the crown over their contentious Separatist beliefs.

By 1619, the Pilgrim's painstaking diplomacy campaign had finally paid off. "At last, after all these occurrences, and their long waiting, they had a patent granted them and confirmed under the Virginia Company's seal." [19] It was a huge step forward in their goal of reaching America, but there was little time to celebrate. Obtaining royal permission and a patent only got them so far—the next big question was how to finance it. A sailing expedition across the Atlantic Ocean was expensive. What the Pilgrims needed now was *money*—a lot of it.

THE MERCHANT ADVENTURERS

By the following year, word of the church's plans reached a group of London investors known as the Merchant Adventurers, and an agent of the company traveled to Leiden and presented an offer to the church. "He and his backers would pay for the necessary trans-Atlantic ship, its crew, provisions for the voyage, and whatever was necessary until the colonists were established. In return, they would work four days a week for the company, producing profits by offshore fishing and fur trapping, and be allowed to work two days for themselves—with no work on the Sabbath. At the end of seven years, their land and houses would become their private property."[20] The congregation was elated. They believed the offer was the very provision they had been praying for, and the church agreed to a contract with the Merchant Adventurers.

But when the company later revised its terms—requiring the Pilgrims to work *six* days a week instead of four, keeping only *half* of their homes and property after seven years—the congregation became indignant. Decrying these new terms as "fitter for thieves and bondslaves than honest men," the church instructed their representatives in London to reject the new contract.[21] What happened next would play a crucial role in determining the final passenger list for the expedition and prove to be an economic thorn in the colony's side for decades to come.

> "To leave for America, the Pilgrims needed the King's permission, a legal land patent, and enough money to finance the entire endeavor— all of which seemed impossibly out of reach."

BELOW: *Dutch marine painter Abraham Storck depicts Amsterdam's busy harbor.*

STRANGERS ONBOARD

Instead of refusing the contract, Robert Cushman impulsively accepted the new terms on behalf of the church. Fearing it would be their last opportunity to strike a deal, Cushman overstepped his authority and even concealed the matter for a time to prevent any further delays—actions that "afterwards caused much trouble and contention." [22] However well-intentioned, Cushman's decision caused a huge backlash in the church. When word of the new contract terms reached the congregation, many who had originally agreed to make the journey refused to go. To bolster the church's lagging numbers, the Merchant Adventurers began to actively solicit new passengers in England. These late recruits, who would be called *"Strangers"* by the Pilgrims, joined the voyage to pursue adventure and opportunity in the new world. While some may have been sympathetic to the Pilgrim's plight, these Strangers did not share the Pilgrim's faith—or their quest for religious freedom. This late influx of passengers would alter the expedition significantly and have broad implications for the Pilgrims in their new colony.

ABOVE: *In "Embarkation of the Pilgrims," artist Robert Walter Weir meticulously researched the written accounts, costume records, and documented history to portray an authentic scene of the Pilgrims leaving Holland for America. At center, Elder William Brewster holds a Geneva Bible as Pastor Robinson leads the congregation in a final prayer.*

LEAVING HOLLAND

After prayer and reflection, the church was still willing to leave for America—but not all could afford to go. Many in the church, such as 30-year-old William Bradford, sold their homes and personal belongings to finance the journey. It was decided that Pastor Robinson would remain in Holland with the majority of the congregation, many of whom were older in years, and Elder William Brewster would accompany those who were leaving. Once a new settlement was established, it was agreed that Pastor Robinson and the remaining members of the congregation would follow—plans that for Robinson, never personally materialized. Although subsequent ships would bring more Pilgrims to Plymouth Colony—including Pastor Robinson's son Isaac onboard the *Anne* in 1623—Robinson himself never set foot in the new world. The Pilgrims were ready to go.

"At length after much discussion everything was got ready. A small ship was bought and fitted out in Holland, intended to help transport them, and then to remain in the country for fishing and other such pursuits as might benefit the colony. Another ship was hired at London, of about 180 tons." [23] On July 22, 1620, the entire church gathered in the seaport town of Delftshaven for a final, tearful goodbye. From there, the departing members boarded the *Speedwell* for England, where they joined the rest of the waiting passengers onboard their second ship, the *Mayflower*. Once united, both vessels would sail to America in tandem—or at least that was the plan. On August 5, 1620, the *Speedwell* and *Mayflower* left the harbor of Southhampton, England, bound for America. They would not get far.

Shortly after they set sail, the *Speedwell* took on water. They stopped in Dartmouth for repairs, but could find nothing wrong. Once they resumed their journey, the *Speedwell* continued to leak. Stopping a second time for repairs, they determined "no special leak could be found, but it was judged to be the general weakness of the ship, and that she would not prove equal to the voyage. Upon which it was resolved to dismiss her, and part of the company, and proceed with the other ship; which, though it caused great discouragement, was put into execution." [24] Troubleshooting a leaky *Speedwell* caused weeks of delay, and some began to doubt their prospects for success. Many onboard, especially those with young children, had become weak and discouraged—and some were unwilling to continue.

"So after they had taken out such provisions as the other ship could well stow, and decided what persons to send back, they made another sad parting."[25] The Pilgrim's brave expedition to the new world was now reduced by half. The remaining passengers and cargo were reorganized onto the *Mayflower,* and the Pilgrims set sail for America on September 6, 1620. The *Mayflower* spent over nine weeks at sea with Captain Christopher Jones at the helm before sighting land. For 66 days, not including the four weeks already spent addressing a leaky *Speedwell,* the Pilgrims lived on the "tween" deck—a middle deck of the ship that yielded 5-foot ceilings and very little room to move around. There was no privacy and little escape from the prying eyes and ears of others. For many onboard, the constant rolling and dipping of the ship caused horrible seasickness—with all its common side effects. There were no bathrooms, no showers, and the vessel was perpetually damp from outside water constantly leaking in. Over thirty of the *Mayflower's* passengers were young energetic children, who—along with the rest of the Pilgrims—spent their days and nights wedged into a space slightly longer than a tennis court. The journey was simply unimaginable.

LEFT: *In England, a stone etched with "Mayflower 1620" marks the harbor where the Pilgrims departed for America.*

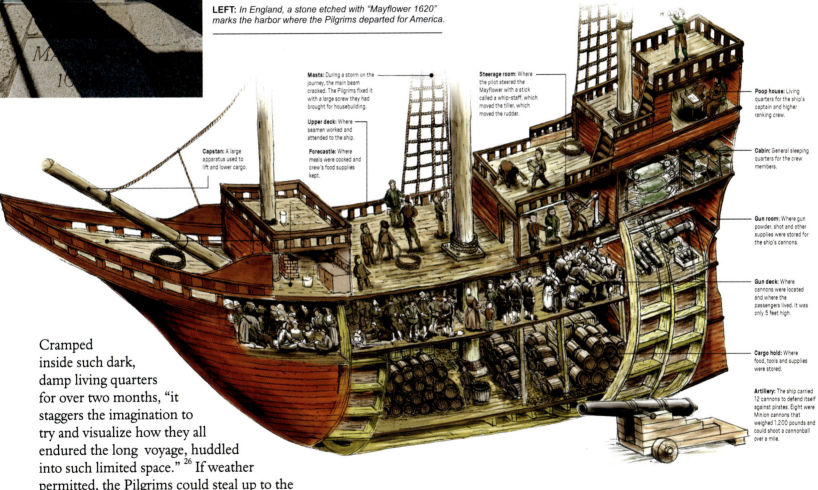

Cramped inside such dark, damp living quarters for over two months, "it staggers the imagination to try and visualize how they all endured the long voyage, huddled into such limited space."[26] If weather permitted, the Pilgrims could steal up to the main deck for moments of fresh air and sunshine—but in bad weather it was far too dangerous. Bradford wrote about the violent storms they encountered at sea, recalling "winds were so fierce and the seas so high, as they could not bear a knot of sail, but were forced to hull (to heave or lay-to under very short sail and drift with the wind) for divers days together."[27] After a leaky *Speedwell* delayed their start, it was November before the *Mayflower* finally reached land—by then the coastline was already frozen and blanketed by snow. Sailing through the frigid waters of Cape Cod Bay, Bradford wrote how "the spray of the sea froze on their coats like glass."[28] When the *Mayflower* finally dropped anchor in Plymouth harbor, it was the middle of December. Her passengers were cold, weary, and malnourished. As the Pilgrims went ashore to start building shelters on land, it wasn't long before many became sick.

ABOVE/BELOW: *Built in 1920 by the General Society of Mayflower Descendants, the Sarcophagus contains the remains of all who died that first winter at Plymouth Colony.*

Of the 102 passengers, only 51 survived the first year at Plymouth Colony. For this small band of people, such losses are difficult to comprehend. During that first brutal winter, two or three people often died in a single day. Four entire families were lost completely. After surviving the treacherous voyage across a "vast and furious ocean," more than a dozen men lost their wives to illness after safely reaching land.[29] The rising death toll was incessant, and the Pilgrims buried their loved ones at night in unmarked graves to prevent any onlookers from calculating the staggering loss of life. As the colony cared for the sick and buried its dead—it's hard to imagine that many didn't simply become numb with grief.

Today, these Pilgrims are memorialized in a Sarcophagus on Cole's Hill overlooking the Plymouth waterfront. Bearing the names of all who died that first winter, it honors those who endured unimaginable hardships to pursue freedom in the new world. Just as "one small candle may light a thousand… to our whole nation, " the principles of faith and liberty that established Plymouth Colony would lay the foundation for America—and in time, become enshrined in her founding documents.[30]

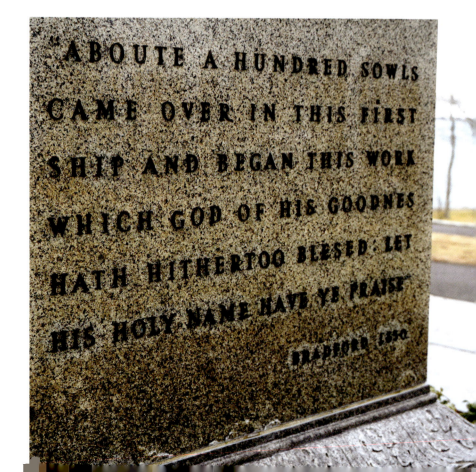

THE PILGRIM SOCIETY

Two hundred years later, in 1820, the town of Plymouth was busy making plans to celebrate the bicentennial anniversary of this historic Pilgrim landing. A small group of citizens, many of who were direct descendants of these first Pilgrims themselves, gathered one evening to consider "the expediency of forming a Society to commemorate the Landing of the Pilgrims."[31] From this meeting the Pilgrim Society emerged, for the stated purpose of "procuring in the town of Plymouth a suitable lot or piece of ground for… a monument to perpetuate the memory of the virtues, the enterprise and the unparalleled suffering of their ancestors who first settled in that ancient town."[32]

As the first order of business, the Society began raising funds to build a public meeting hall with enough space to house a library and display Pilgrim-related antiquities. A parcel of land was eventually purchased for this new building, which was aptly named Pilgrim Hall. On September 1, 1824, the cornerstone was laid, and Pilgrim Hall was dedicated with a plaque that read:

> "In grateful memory of our ancestors who exiled themselves from their native country, for the sake of religion, and here successfully laid the foundation of Freedom and Empire December xxii. A.D. MDCXX. Their descendants, the Pilgrim Society, have raised this edifice, August xxxi, A.D. MDCCCXXIV. A. Parris, Architect - J. & A. S. Taylor, Builders - H. Morse, Sc."[33]

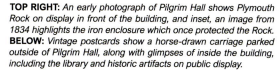

TOP RIGHT: *An early photograph of Pilgrim Hall shows Plymouth Rock on display in front of the building, and inset, an image from 1834 highlights the iron enclosure which once protected the Rock.*
BELOW: *Vintage postcards show a horse-drawn carriage parked outside of Pilgrim Hall, along with glimpses of inside the building, including the library and historic artifacts on public display.*

PILGRIM HALL

By late December, work had progressed far enough for the Society to hold its first meeting inside the newly constructed Pilgrim Hall. However, they were unable to complete the hall's entrance according to the architect's design. In a foreshadowing of problems to come—the Trustees soon learned that building with granite was expensive. It wasn't until 1921, a full 97 years later, that the Society replaced the six wooden columns of its Greek-inspired Doric portico with Quincy granite. By then Pilgrim Hall was established as the single most important depository of historical Pilgrim artifacts in the nation. It held an impressive collection of items from the earliest days of Plymouth Colony, including Plymouth's most famous Rock.

Sometime before 1774, Plymouth Rock was removed from its harbor location and placed in the center of Town Square. There, "Plymouth Rock was visited reverently… but its exposed location also enabled souvenir hunters. Fragments were knocked off the boulder… so that in time it was rounded off and assumed its familiar shape."[34] To safeguard their prized relic from further damage, the town relocated it to the entrance of Pilgrim Hall, and Plymouth Rock was entrusted to the Society's care. It was housed in a circular iron enclosure at the entrance until 1880 when it was moved to a granite canopy at the waterfront, effectively returning Plymouth Rock to its original home. Today, Pilgrim Hall is better known as Pilgrim Hall Museum, and "hosts the world's most significant collection of original Pilgrim possessions, with three galleries of authentic artifacts, paintings, sculpture, rare documents and books," including Governor William Bradford's Bible, the sword of Captain Myles Standish, and a painting of Edward Winslow—the only known portrait of a Pilgrim painted from life.[35]

A DESIGN COMPETITION

By 1849, members of the Pilgrim Society were impatient. Their northern neighbors had already completed a magnificent Bunker Hill monument in Boston, and they were eager to accomplish a similar feat in Plymouth. In a sweeping vote, the members declared it "expedient to erect a monument upon, or near, the Rock on which the Pilgrims landed," and urged Trustees to immediately secure an architect.[36] To accomplish this goal, a competition of sorts was devised. Placing ads in newspapers across the region, the Trustees invited designers to submit plans for a "granite monument" to honor the Pilgrim Fathers in Plymouth. A cash prize of $300 was offered for the winning design, an amount equal to $10,000 in the year 2021. Several proposals were reviewed before the Trustees selected a winner, and the contest prize was awarded to a team of New York architects named Zucker and Asboth. Everything was poised to move forward until a Boston native by the name of Hammatt Billings intervened—and his colossal vision for a Pilgrim monument in Plymouth would change everything.

ABOVE: *An 1854 notice solicits artists and architects.*

HAMMATT BILLINGS

As an artist and architect, Billings was known for his keen intellect and sound judgement. On a work site one morning, Billings objected to the poor quality of bricks that had been selected for construction. The contractor balked at his criticism, exclaiming, *"What do you know of brick? I have dealt in the article for twenty-five years!"* Unfazed, Billings quickly replied: *"Did it take you twenty-five years to learn the quality of a brick?"*

Source: Old And New, Vol. XI, Jan.1875

ARCHITECT HAMMATT BILLINGS

Often compared to Michaelangelo for his wide range of talent and artistic versatility, Hammatt Billings "saturated the field of design in mid-nineteenth-century Boston."[37] An accomplished painter, illustrator, designer, and architect—Billings was considered a rare talent in many different mediums of art. He was a gifted illustrator, and his work regularly appeared in popular periodicals such as the *Boston Almanac* and *Gleason's (later Ballou's) Pictorial Drawing-Room Companion*. Billings created illustrations for over 250 book titles by authors such as Harriet Beecher Stowe, Louisa May Alcott, and Charles Dickens, and he was best known for his original work in *Uncle Tom's Cabin* and *Little Women*.

Billings was mighty with a pencil, and "his tireless production suggests that he was one of the most sought-after illustrators of his generation in the Boston area."[38] His natural genius for sketching easily lent itself to drafting, and "by the early 1850s he was an established architect and designer in the city… not only sought after by patrons but envied by his peers."[39] His talents placed him in great demand for professional collaborations, including partnerships with his younger brother, Joseph. Respected throughout the city, Billings' architectural portfolio included notable commissions for Boston's Athenaeum, the Boston Museum, Church of the Saviour, and Wellesley College.

ABOVE: *An early watercolor by Billings depicts the Biblical figure of Joseph inside of Pharoah's court.*

ABOVE: *Billings designed the original Boston Museum on Tremont Street, which stood until 1903 before it was demolished. Here, the original interior is shown with its intricate carvings, columns, and sweeping stairwell.*

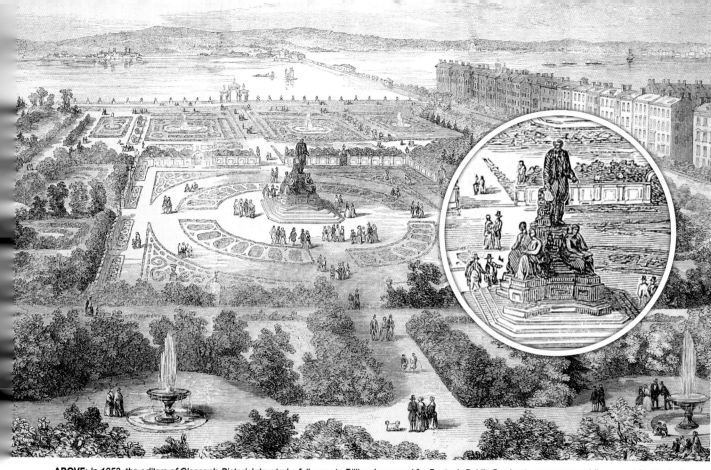

At left is Billings' 1853 proposal for a statue honoring Congressman Daniel Webster in Boston's Public Garden. Although his plan was not realized, the idea would become a remarkable prototype for Billings' creation of the Forefathers Monument in Plymouth.

Can you spot the similarities?

ABOVE: *In 1853, the editors of Gleason's Pictorial devoted a full page to Billings' proposal for Boston's Public Garden to encourage public support for his design.*

> Billings saturated the field of design in mid-nineteenth-century Boston. No one else comes to mind who was so highly praised in so many departments of art, whose presence so thoroughly permeated the popular culture of the period, who served such a broad constituency, whose talents showed itself in so many different lights. A sizable portion of the population of nineteenth-century Boston that read books or periodicals, attended church, school, or the theater, buried its dead, celebrated civic festivals, envisioned the past or current events, attended concerts or art exhibitions, sang songs, or lived the commercial life of the city could not do so without encountering something of Billings's presence.
>
> Source: *Accomplished In All Departments Of Art* by James F. O'Gorman

A GRAND DESIGN

Billings also frequently designed funeral monuments and memorials as an artist, and he "labored long and lovingly over the commemorative arts."[40] By the early 1850's, Billings had become intrigued with the design of monumental public art. He proposed a sizable monument to the Minutemen at Lexington Green, along with a massive statue of Congressman Daniel Webster for Boston's Public Garden. Although neither proposal came to fruition, his fascination with significant outdoor monuments continued. Over the next several years, Billings became preoccupied with sketches of what close friends called *"his grand design."*

This zeal to produce a magnificent public monument for the ages eventually led Billings to contact the Pilgrim Society in Plymouth. In a series of letters written to the Trustees, Billings presented a compelling proposal for not just one monument—*but two*. Along with his sweeping vision for a gigantic Pilgrim monument in Plymouth, Billings also offered to design a new canopy for Plymouth Rock. Tipping the scales further, he boldly agreed to "raise the money himself, indemnifying the Society against loss, if the trustees would accept his own design."[41] And what a design it was. Towering over 150 feet high, Billings' ambitious plan for a Pilgrim monument was *colossal*.

A MONUMENT FOR THE AGES

In Billings' proposal, the central figure of *Faith* loomed over four seated figures below her to represent *Morality, Law, Education,* and *Freedom* (later changed to Liberty.) On *Faith*'s octagonal pedestal, massive panels displayed the names of those who sailed on the *Mayflower*. Large marble reliefs at the base depicted pivotal moments in the Pilgrim story.

Billings designed a special chamber inside its massive base to publicly display historical Pilgrim records and artifacts. Inside this museum, a stairwell led visitors to an outdoor observation deck situated at the feet of *Faith*. From this platform, guests could see all of Plymouth harbor and observe the various "places of interest connected with the history of the forefathers."[42] As an architect, Billings' design aspirations ran well ahead of his time. As initially drawn, his magnificent tribute to the Pilgrim forefathers stood taller than New York's *Statue of Liberty*—a monument that would not be conceived until 1865—a full ten years later.

Although the Pilgrim Society had already announced their contest winners, Billings' proposition was compelling. A crucial clause in the contest rules allowed them the right to refuse any final design, and many Trustees were conflicted over how to proceed. Eventually, Billings' grand proposal for not just one but *two* monuments—along with his offer to raise all needed funds—won them over. They awarded the $300 cash prize to winning architects Zucker and Asboth but gave the contract to Billings instead.

ABOVE: *An 1873 Pilgrim Society membership certificate illustrated by Billings demonstrate the grand scale of his original proposal for the monument, and highlight key Pilgrim events such as the signing of the Mayflower Compact.*

On May 23, 1855, the Pilgrim Society hired Hammatt Billings as their architect and project superintendent. For his part, Billings agreed to build a canopy for Plymouth Rock in four years and to complete the Forefathers Monument in just twelve. After years of dashed hopes and failed proposals, Billings was finally poised to achieve his dream of building a soaring public memorial for the ages. But while the Forefathers Monument would one day be viewed as his signature achievement, Billings himself would not live to see its completed design. As news of their partnership was formally announced to the public, Billings' handcrafted press release heralded what was to come.

"**THE NATIONAL MONUMENT TO THE FOREFATHERS**, which is just about to be commenced under the auspices of the Pilgrim Society, is intended to be the grandest work of the kind in the world. Raised in commemoration of the great starting-point in our history, it is the idea to make it, as far as possible, worthy of the great event which it will record. In size it will be the greatest of modern works, and only equaled by those vast monuments of Egyptian power and grandeur which remain to us, the most wonderful triumphs of mere mechanical power. It is to be built of massive blocks of granite, and will be eighty feet at the base, and a little over one hundred and fifty feet high. The plan of the principal pedestal is an octagon, with four small and four large faces; from the small faces project four buttresses or wing pedestals. On the main pedestal stands a figure of Faith. One foot rests upon the Forefather's Rock; in her left hand she holds an open Bible; with the right uplifted, she points to heaven. Looking downward, as to those she is addressing, she seems to call them to trust in a higher power. This figure is to be of granite, and will be seventy feet high.

On each of the four smaller or wing pedestals is a seated figure; they are emblematic of the principles upon which the Pilgrims proposed to found their Commonwealth. The first of these is Morality. She holds the Decalogue in her left and the scroll of Revelation in her right hand; her look is upward towards the impersonation of the Spirit of Religion above. In a niche, on one side of her throne, is a Prophet, and in the other one of the Evangelists. The second of these figures is Law. On one side of his seat is Justice; on the other Mercy. The third is Education. In the niche, on one side of her seat, is Wisdom, ripe with years; on the other, Youth led by Experience. The fourth figure is Freedom (Liberty). On one side Peace rests under his protection; on the other, Tyranny is overthrown by his prowess. Upon the faces of these projecting pedestals are alto-reliefs representing scenes from the history of the Pilgrims. The first is the departure from Delft-haven; the second, the signing of the social compact; the third, the landing at Plymouth; the fourth, the first treaty with the Indians. These reliefs are to be in marble, as susceptible of greater delicacy of treatment. The four figures on these pedestals are to be of granite, each thirty-four feet high. The figures in the panels eight feet.

On each of the four large faces of the main pedestal is to be a large panel for records. That in front will contain the names of all who came over in the Mayflower; behind, the events of the voyage. On one side, the events previous to sailing from Delft-haven; on the other, early events of the colony. Below these are to be smaller panels, to contain the dedication of the monument, names of officers of the Pilgrim Society, etc., and such other records as may be considered of sufficient consequence. Within the monument will be a chamber twenty-six feet in diameter, with a stone stair leading up to the platform, upon which stands the principal figure. From this platform, which will be over eighty feet above the entrance at the ground, all the principal localities in the early history of the colony of Plymouth may be seen almost at a glance. The anchorage-ground of the Mayflower, the location of the Rock where the first Pilgrims landed, Captain's Hill, at Duxbury, etc. Around the monument, a space of nine acres, making it a fine square, is to be kept open forever."

Source: *Pilgrim Memorials and Guide To Plymouth* by William Shaw Russell

A NATIONAL FUNDRAISING CAMPAIGN

Work began immediately. Billings hired a financial agent to oversee all fundraising receipts and launched "a nationwide, grassroots effort through a system of state or regional representatives" to collect donations for the Monument Fund.[43] Billings created a printed circular to solicit donations, and copies of this flyer were distributed across the nation. In it, all Americans were invited to "contribute something towards the first great monumental record ever built by a nation to commemorate… the memory of men who sought a new land, not in pursuit of wealth, power, or glory, but for the free exercise of their religious faith and the establishment of the principles of universal self-government."[44]

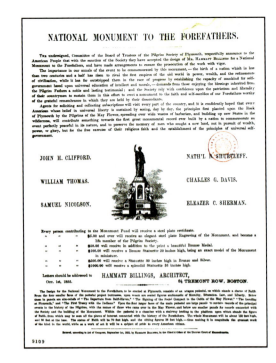

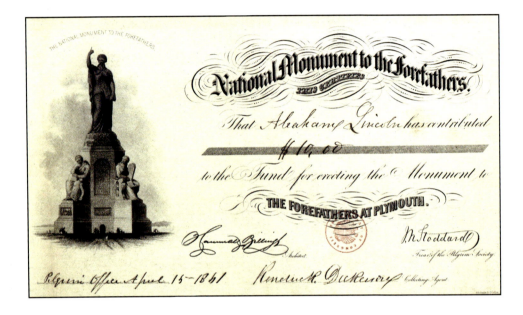

ABOVE: *The original flyer circulated to announce plans for the National Monument to the Forefathers.*
LEFT: *The receipt for President Lincoln's personal donation to the Monument Fund is displayed with his personal papers at the Library of Congress.*
BELOW: *An 1864 edition of the Illustrated Pilgrim Memorial, which was designed by Billings and distributed nationwide for a donation of 25-cents.*

In 1861, President Lincoln donated $10 to the Monument Fund—which would equal nearly $300 in 2021. Two years later, in 1863, Lincoln honored the Pilgrims again with a Presidential *Proclamation of Thanksgiving*. In it, he fervently declared that America's bounties were "so constantly enjoyed that we are prone to forget the source from which they come" and encouraged citizens "to set apart and observe the last Thursday of November next as a day of thanksgiving and praise to our beneficent Father who dwelleth in the heavens."[45] With this proclamation, the Pilgrim practice of setting aside a day for public prayer and thanks to God became enshrined in the distinctly American holiday known as Thanksgiving.

Throughout the monument's fundraising campaign, Billings' artistic talents were on full display. Each donation of $5 or more received a print engraving of the monument made from a steel plate and a certificate of membership to the Pilgrim Society. For a $50 contribution, donors received a handsome bronze medal crafted by Billings. More significant donations garnered a cast metal statuette of the monument, either in bronze or silver, ranging from 20 to 36-inches high. In support of the effort, Billings also published *The Illustrated Pilgrim Memorial*, a newsmagazine filled with Pilgrim articles and illustrations that sold for 25 cents. Conceived by Billings, it became a savvy marketing tool to promote the idea of a Pilgrim monument in Plymouth and generate nationwide support.

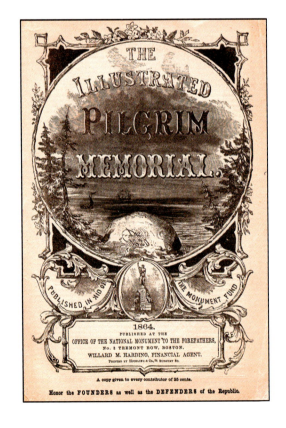

BELOW: *In 1853, Gleason's Pictorial Magazine ran several illustrations of the Pilgrim celebration in Plymouth. Here, one sketch depicts the huge crowds that gathered for ceremony and processionals to honor the Pilgrims and promote the Monument Fund.*

PILGRIM CELEBRATION AT PLYMOUTH, MASS., AUGUST 1, 1853.

> In response to criticism that his proposal for a Pilgrim monument was too grand, Billings replied:
>
> "No monument can be on a scale of too great grandeur, nor can it be made too imperishable, to express to the full the sense of obligation which is felt towards them, and the grateful affection with which their memory is cherished."
>
> Source: *Accomplished In All Departments Of Art* by James F. O'Gorman

As efforts to promote the Monument Fund continued everywhere, "the high point of this campaign was a celebration held in Plymouth in August, 1853. A great tent was set up on the Training Green to accommodate the large crowds which thronged to Plymouth, and *Gleason's Pictorial Magazine* ran a series of prints illustrating the activities."[46]

LAYING OF THE CORNERSTONE

Contributions came in slowly, but by 1859, enough progress was made for work to begin. On August 2, 1859, thousands of dignitaries and supporters came to Plymouth from across the region to celebrate the grand cornerstone-laying ceremony of the National Monument to the Forefathers and the canopy for Plymouth Rock. The ceremony featured public prayers and processionals, followed by a seated dinner for almost 3,000 people. Several speeches followed dinner, along with a formal letter of congratulations from President James Buchanan that was read aloud to an enthralled audience. The exuberant spirit of the day was articulated in the words of the Society's President, Richard Warren, who declared: "No victory has ever been so pregnant in its consequences; no event in the human story, save that which occurred at Bethlehem, has produced so vast a revolution in the destinies of the human race, as the emigration of the Pilgrims of the Mayflower. It is worthy then... to erect a memorial of gratitude, which shall embody in its design the leading characteristics of the Pilgrim mind."[47]

A photograph of Billing's 1867 Plymouth Rock canopy closely resembles his original sketch, including the granite scallop shells which are often associated with the Pilgrims as a symbol of pilgrimage.

ABOVE: *Plymouth Rock's original stood for over fifty years until it was replaced by the current structure in 1919. In this picture, the large granite shells from Billing's original design can clearly be seen. Today, these surviving shells mark the start of the stone footpath leading up to the Forefathers Monument.* **RIGHT:** *An early sketch of Billings' proposed canopy previews the finished work that was built at the Plymouth waterfront.* **BELOW:** *These large granite shells are some of the few remaining elements of Billings' first canopy.*

PLYMOUTH ROCK CANOPY

The new canopy for Plymouth Rock was completed in 1867 and became a striking addition to the waterfront. The 30-foot-tall structure consisted of "three-quarter reeded columns of the Tuscan order, standing on pedestals," and its roof was adorned with granite shells to symbolize "the pilgrim character of the enterprise of the Fathers."[48] It stood for years with mixed reviews until 1919, when it was torn down to make way for the modern structure designed by the architectural firm of McKim, Mead, and White. Before it was demolished, the granite shells on the roof were mysteriously salvaged. Today, these shells line the path up to the monument as some of the only surviving elements of the original structure.

With the first part of his contract completed, Billings could now give his full attention to the Forefathers project. However, post-war inflation had spiked, raising serious concerns over the ability to finance such a massive public endeavor. By 1874, the entire project was in jeopardy. To save it, Billings reluctantly conceded to the financial realities of the day. Returning to his studio, he modified the original scale of his grand design—reducing the monument's size by nearly *half*. Although his first proposal imagined a soaring memorial that stood an astounding 153-feet-high, Billings' revised plan called for a far more modest — *and affordable*—81-foot-tall structure. These last-minute design reductions eliminated earlier plans for a museum and observation deck. When Billings presented his modified proposal to the Trustees, they quickly accepted his offer—eager to move forward with a design more within their financial reach. This exchange would mark Billings' final input on the project before his unexpected death later that year.

After months of poor health, Hammatt Billings passed away on November 14, 1874, during a visit with his brother Henry in New York. He was at the height of his architectural career. Death notices flooded in from across the region, each lauding his talent and generosity. The *Boston Daily Advertiser* eulogized Billings as "truly a great artist... (who) had that rare quality of being ever ready to recognize merit in others. He was... generous even when he could ill afford it. Many a young genius has been given his first start toward the realization of his aspirations by the kindly aid of Hammatt Billings."[49]

Death of Hammatt Billings.
A despatch from New York states that Hammatt Billings, the well known artist and architect, died in that city on Saturday. Mr. Billings was especially well known in this city, where he had a wide circle of admiring friends. His drawings for the illustration of many popular works have made his name a household word where art is appreciated, and many fine structures have been the work of his directing genius and skilful hand. Mr. Billings was fifty-seven years old, and had been ill about a week.

ABOVE: *A newspaper announcement of Billings' death.*

In their obituary, the *Boston Daily Globe* wrote: "Mr. Billings was especially well known in this city, where he had a wide circle of admiring friends. His drawings for the illustration of many popular works have made him a household word where art is appreciated, and many fine structures have been the work of his directing genius and skillful hand."[50] After the loss of their visionary designer, the Society approached Joseph Billings to continue in his brother's work. Relying on Hammatt's original sketches, Joseph collaborated with other artists and sculptors to bring his brother's vision for the monument to life. Joseph supervised the carving of *Faith* in 1877 and continued as project manager until he died in 1880.

BELOW: *A view of the modern portico over Plymouth Rock at dusk. To learn more about the historical origins of this famous American landmark, see page 58.*

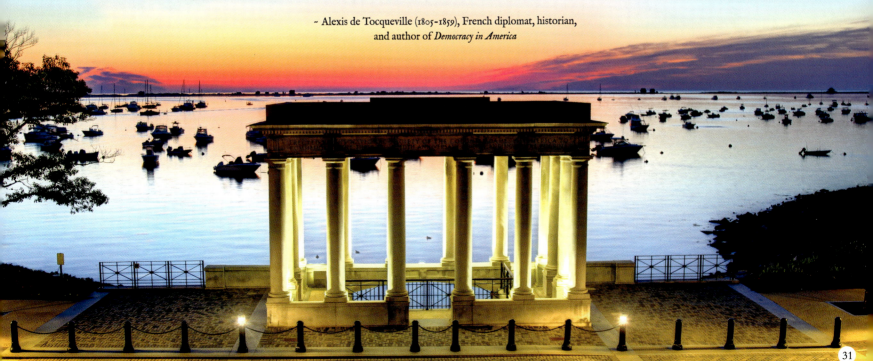

"This Rock has become an object of veneration in the United States. I have seen bits of it carefully preserved in several towns of the Union. Does not this sufficiently show how all human power and greatness are entirely in the soul? Here is a stone which the feet of a few poor outcasts pressed for an instant, and this stone becomes famous; it is treasured by a great nation, a fragment is prized as a relic."

~ Alexis de Tocqueville (1805-1859), French diplomat, historian,
and author of *Democracy in America*

TOP LEFT: *Sands Quarry was one of several quarries owned by Maine's Bodwell Granite Company, and where the monument's 700-ton pedestal was likely produced in 1875.* **TOP RIGHT:** *An early photograph of men working outside of Bodwell's cutting sheds in Vinalhaven, Maine, dated from 1903.*

BODWELL GRANITE COMPANY

With a new design in hand and Hammett's brother Joseph Billings at the helm, the Society hired the Bodwell Granite Company in Maine to carve the monument's pedestal. Bodwell operated several quarries on the island of Vinalhaven at the time and was one of the nation's top producers of granite. Bodwell was famous for supplying granite to many high-profile projects such as the Brooklyn Bridge, the Washington Monument, Boston's Court House, the Cathedral of St. John the Divine in New York, and the Congressional Library in Washington, D.C. Even after Billings reduced the design, the size of the monument's pedestal was substantial—it stood 45 feet high and weighed over 700 tons. Bodwell completed the work in November of 1875, and the pedestal was delivered to Plymouth and installed the following year. Once the pedestal was in place, attention shifted to the creation of each of the monument's five allegorical figures. To begin, the cost of carving *Faith* was sponsored by the Honorable Oliver Ames, Jr., a railroad executive and former Massachusetts State Senator (1852-1857).[51] A noted philanthropist and Plymouth native, Ames generously offered to underwrite the cost of producing *Faith*—by far the monument's most prominent and expensive figure. With funding secured, the Society commissioned the Hallowell Granite Company in Hallowell, Maine, to create *Faith*, and quarrying for the project began in June of 1876.

HALLOWELL GRANITE WORKS

Known throughout the east coast for their superior granite and expert craftsmen, Hallowell Granite Works was a perfect choice to produce the central figure of *Faith*. Hallowell's beautiful white granite "was light and fine grained, with a high percentage of feldspar which made it easily worked in the quarry and under the chisel. When dressed it was almost as white as marble, and when polished its surface glittered like diamonds."[52] Hallowell's stunning white granite was brought to life by master artisans who came to America from Italy, Spain, England, and Scotland—and its skilled carvers and stonecutters were renowned for their exquisite statuary work. Many men employed by Hallowell had previously worked in the famous marble quarries of Carrara, Italy—a favorite of Michelangelo—and were considered unrivaled in their work.

BOTTOM LEFT: *A photograph of the Hallowell's quarry, where the granite slabs used to create Faith were quarried. This interior vantage point offers a direct view of the essential tools of the granite quarry—the mine, railroad tracks, and cranes that were essential tools of the industry.* **BOTTOM RIGHT:** *Huge pieces of granite are moved from the quarry to the carving shed.*

ABOVE LEFT/RIGHT: Rare photographs of stonecutters at work inside the cutting sheds, surrounded by the tools of their craft. **BOTTOM:** At a quarry in Vinalhaven, Maine, carvers are captured working outside near railroad tracks, close to a rail-mounted steam derrick (shown in back) which would lift massive pieces of finished granite for delivery.

The level of skill and artistry that was required to create *Faith* was immense. Hallowell awarded the contract to famed Spanish sculptor Joseph Archie, considered at the time to be one of the finest carvers in the land. Working with his team of sculptors, Archie used scale models and illustrations to replicate *Faith's* 36-foot-tall likeness. When the statue was finally completed, her finished form consisted of 14 pieces of granite weighing 180 tons.

Faith was completed on July 19, 1877, and the spectacle of her year-long construction generated significant local interest. Because of the project's notoriety, Hallowell placed *Faith* on public display in their company yard for several days before she was delivered to Plymouth. Thousands flocked to see the exhibit.

It cost $32,300 to construct the statue of *Faith,* an amount which would exceed $800,000 in the year 2021. In the end, the bill was settled by the estate of Oliver Ames. Exactly five months to the day before *Faith* was installed on August 9, 1877, Oliver Ames passed away. Sadly, *Faith's* generous benefactor would share the same fate as her architect—and neither would live to see her finished form.

Over the next decade, the remaining figures were completed and set in place. *Morality* was installed in 1878, *Education* was established in 1881, and *Law* and *Liberty* were both seated in 1888.

ABOVE: *A rare picture of Faith inside Hallowell's cutting yard. The job of carving Faith was assigned to Joseph Archie, who is seen here standing on Faith's shoulder above his working crew. The carvers used scale models and drawings to reproduce Faith's 36-foot tall likeness. Several pictures are visible around the work site, which were no doubt used as a visual reference as they worked.*

From the signing of their first contract with Hammatt Billings in 1855, it took the Pilgrim Society over three decades to achieve their goal of building a national monument to honor the Pilgrims. The final cost of the monument and its surrounding grounds came to $135,000—an impressive sum given the challenging financial climate during the Civil War. In what amounted to a 34-year-long fund-raising campaign, the monument was eventually achieved through private donations and public funds received from Massachusetts, Connecticut, and the United States Congress. Adjusted for inflation, the cost to produce the Forefathers Monument in 2021 would be well over four million dollars.

DONORS FROM NEAR AND FAR

The final list of donors included over 11,000 individuals, societies, and associations from across the nation and abroad. Donations came in from nearly each of the 38 states ratified at the time, including Alabama, California, Connecticut, District of Columbia, Illinois, Indiana, Iowa, Kansas, Kentucky, Louisiana, Maine, Maryland, Massachusetts, Michigan, Minnesota, Missouri, Nebraska, Nevada, New Hampshire, New Jersey, New York, Ohio, Pennsylvania, Rhode Island, South Carolina, Tennessee, Vermont, Virginia, Washington, and Wisconsin. Donations also arrived from Canadian territories such as New Brunswick and Nova Scotia and as far off as France, England, and Africa. In a fitting tribute to the English heritage of the Pilgrims at Plymouth Colony, an 1864 edition of the *Illustrated Pilgrim Memorial* noted that the very first donation to the Monument Fund was made by the Old Pilgrim Church in Southwark, England.

ABOVE: *In the foreground, numbered slabs of granite wait to be carved.*

ABOVE: *Early photographs of the monument's construction as each of the lower figures were installed. Morality (**left**) was the first statue to be set in place after Faith was installed on her base. The figure of Education (**center**) was the third statue to be placed, followed by the final installation of Liberty (**right**) and Law (blocked from view), in October and November of 1888.*

THE MONUMENT IS DEDICATED

On Thursday, August 1, 1889, over 12,000 visitors—nearly double the town's population—descended on Plymouth for the monument's dedication festivities. All schools were closed for the day to enable the children to participate in the parade, and regional train schedules were increased to help shuttle the massive crowds. The entire town participated in some form or fashion. Professional decorators from Boston and Hartford were hired to build grand arches throughout Plymouth, and the downtown streets were awash in colorful bunting. Although summer showers fell throughout the day, the rain did nothing to dampen the crowd's spirits. The dedication of the Forefathers Monument began promptly at 9:30 a.m., and reporters and sketch artists were on hand to record the spectacle. The Grand Chaplain opened with an invocation, followed by numerous speeches and proclamations to mark the occasion. The dedication ceremony concluded with a closing benediction, after which the assembled crowd sang a rousing rendition of the hymn *"America."*

From there, thousands lined the streets of Plymouth to take in the colorful parade. The processional included twenty horse-drawn carriages filled with dignitaries and guests, followed by local fire divisions, battery teams, and mounted police. Beginning at Court Street, the parade "wound around a three-mile circuitous route, passing the monument, then returning through town to the waterfront... (and) ending near the depot where a tent had been erected for the dinner."[53] From there, the enthusiastic crowds enjoyed refreshments and outdoor concerts at the harbor where the Pilgrims first disembarked. That evening, nearly two thousand guests—1,978 people to be exact—attended a special dinner banquet that boasted no less than nine speeches from various dignitaries. At dusk, the monument was illuminated by an enormous focus light as fireworks lit the night sky. The day ended with a gala ball, as guests danced late into the evening to the music of a 17-piece band. For everyone who attended, it was a grand celebration of a long-awaited achievement for Plymouth.

ABOVE: *In 1889, Harper's Weekly ran a two-page news article on the dedication ceremony of the "Pilgrim" monument in Plymouth, Massachusetts. The feature included illustrations of the large crowds gathered around the monument that day (above), and depictions of its four seated figures (shown on the opposite page).* **RIGHT:** *An image taken from a glass slide used with a Magic Lantern, an early slide projector developed in the 17th century. Here, the image of a crowd walking up to the monument is remarkably similar to the illustrations featured in Harper's Weekly—complete with top hats, parasols, and horse-drawn carriages. Although the glass slide is undated, the fact that the image was produced commercially for use in a Magic Lantern indicates it captured a significant event of that era. That, combined with other visual references, suggest this is an actual photograph of the crowds that gathered for the dedication of the Forefathers Monument in Plymouth on August 1, 1889.*

"It is our hope that this monument may serve a double purpose. First, let it keep alive in the hearts of later generations the memory of all that our present prosperity has cost; that our ease has been bought with the struggles and privations of many; and that faith and undaunted heroism have entered into the very foundations of our institutions. Let it stand to teach that reverence for the past which is part of every true nature. Only by building on the past can we lift ourselves to higher levels. Let this monument stand, also, as a promise for the future. Let it teach young men that to rightfully reverence the past, they must live for the future, as did those men whose memory we honor today. Prosperity has its own perils no less than adversity. It is sometimes easier to be brave in the face of hardship than to be true in the midst of luxury. How many a man has kept himself honest and hardworking in comparative poverty, who has proved himself unequal to the temptations of sudden wealth. Let this monument say to him who would honor the Pilgrim, that he can rightfully do so only by practicing the Pilgrims' virtues. May it stand through the years to recall the early days of our country, to the minds of all who behold it, and to bear witness to that surpassing power in the human heart, which reckons pain and suffering of little account, when it is pressing forward to the accomplishment of divine ends."

- Opening Invocation of the Dedication Ceremony, Delivered by Rev. Charles A. Skinner, Grand Chaplain, August 1, 1889

ABOVE: *Mature trees now surround the monument, but an 1881 photograph (at right) taken after Education was installed demonstrates its original panoramic views of Plymouth harbor.*

THE MONUMENT THROUGHOUT HISTORY

The Forefathers Monument has gone by many names over the years. In 1854, the Pilgrim Society first solicited designs for a *Pilgrim Monument,* a title that carried through most early publications. In 1889, it was officially dedicated as the *National Monument to the Forefathers*, a formal title which is often shortened to the *Forefathers Monument.* Most locals speak of it self-evidently as "the monument" or mention it by its most prominent figure—and affectionately call her *Faith*. Regardless of formality, the Forefathers Monument is the largest free-standing solid granite monument in the nation. In 1974, it was added to the National Registry of Historic Places (NRHP) for preservation. In 2001, the Pilgrim Society deeded the monument to the Commonwealth of Massachusetts. This historical structure, along with Plymouth Rock, now comprises Pilgrim Memorial State Park.

Originally built on one of the highest hills overlooking Plymouth harbor, a maturing tree line has eclipsed the monument's once panoramic views. Residential development has transformed its former place of prominence into one of curiosity. Yet despite the monument's perplexing location, it "continues to draw an estimated 250,000 visitors every year" in Plymouth, often referred to as "America's Hometown."[54] In recent years, the monument has gained renewed interest in television and film documentaries, including the 2012 film, *Monumental.* Over four hundred years after the Pilgrims landed in 1620, the Forefathers Monument remains a powerful symbol of the Pilgrim legacy. Built to honor the brave men and women who first sailed to America and established self-government at Plymouth Colony, it is an enduring tribute to the people and principles that founded a nation.

THE MONUMENT IN MEMORABILIA

From its jubilant dedication ceremony in 1889 to modern-day observances, the Forefathers Monument has played a significant role in the history of Plymouth, Massachusetts—affectionately referred to as *"America's Hometown."* In early postcards, puzzles, and commemorative coins, the iconic image of *Faith* has become a fixture in town souvenirs and memorabilia.

ABOVE: *A postcard mailer unfolds to reveal colorful highlights of historic "Pilgrim" Plymouth.* **RIGHT:** *Postcards from 1900 to 1960.*

RIGHT: *A 10x15 picture puzzle depicts the "Pilgrim Monument," circa 1950.*

LEFT: *A souvenir juice cup, circa 1970.*

ABOVE: *A rare ceramic plaque of the "National Monument" in Plymouth, circa 1930. It was originally sold at the historic John Alden Gift Shop on the waterfront, established in 1918.*

RIGHT: *A collectible medallion was minted in 1989 to commemorate the 100th anniversary of the Forefathers Monument.*

ABOVE: *Vintage tourism brochures highlight the historic sights of "America's Home Town," circa 1960.*

BELOW: *A miniature jug crafted in Germany for a Plymouth novelty merchant, circa 1900.*

BELOW: *Medals presented to officials and special guests at the monument's dedication ceremonies on August 1, 1889. The number originally struck is unknown, but today these pieces are extremely rare. At left, the medallion pierced with a hole at top suggests it was originally attached to a ribbon to be pinned, or ultimately modified to be worn as jewelry. In 2014, both medallions sold for $440 and $1880 respectively, the difference in price reflecting the quality.*

FRONT: *BACK:*   *FRONT:*   *BACK:*

MAINTENANCE AND REPAIRS

Over the years, exposure to the elements, limited maintenance, and even acts of vandalism have placed the monument in need of repairs. **(1)** In the early 1980's, four of the fingers on *Law's* right hand were broken off, presumably by vandals. **(2)** In 1986, the replacements for these missing fingers were remodeled and installed with pins and epoxy. **(3)** Today, the evidence of this repair is still visible due to the contrasting appearance of the stone.

(4) For the large marble reliefs at the monument's base, prolonged exposure to wind, rain, and salt spray has led to a type of coastal erosion known as salt weathering, or sugaring, which has coarsened the stone's surface and caused a significant loss of detail. Although large glass enclosures once protected these reliefs, years of exposure to the elements have caused irreparable damage. Several faces depicted in the *Pilgrim's Landing* panel are entirely eroded due to salt weathering, and similar damage is visible on other panels. **(5)** A 1906 photograph reveals the glass panels that once covered the marble panels. **(6)** Comparing a vintage postcard against a current picture (inset) reveals the extent of the damage. **(7)** In 1929, the lower panels were cleaned and reset with glass to protect the marble. It is unclear exactly when these glass coverings were abandoned. **(8)** In 1933, the monument was struck during an electrical storm. **(9)** The force of the lightning bolt shifted the pedestal of *Law* by a foot and sent broken chunks of granite flying up to 300 feet away. **(10)** In 1912, four young vandals inflicted such severe damage to the monument that it appeared *Faith* would have to be removed— at great expense—to complete the necessary repairs. In time, the builders were able to devise a solution to repair the monument, which left *Faith* intact.

⑤

⑥

LEFT: *The glass frames which once covered the lower marble panels are clearly visible in a 1906 photograph.* **RIGHT TOP:** *The dramatic extent of the damage is visible when comparing a 1940's postcard with a recent picture of the panel (see above inset). Without intervention, these marble panels will continue to erode over time, and these historic panels' intricate details will be irretrievably lost.*

⑦

FOREFATHERS' MONUMENT AT PLYMOUTH UNDERGOING REPAIRS

Cracks Filled In and Four Great Bas Reliefs Being Cleaned and Reset With Glass

FOREFATHERS' MONUMENT AS IT LOOKS WHILE BEING REPAIRED

⑧

BOLT BADLY DAMAGES STATUE IN PLYMOUTH

Forefathers Monument May Have to Be Taken Down

Special Dispatch to the Globe

PLYMOUTH, April 4—The damage by lightning last night to the National Forefathers' Monument, which stands on Monument Hill and has been a landmark since 1889, was of such a nature that it is believed that the statue will have to be taken down and put up again. Part of the statue of Law—one of four buttresses—will have to be replaced.

Faith is the central figure of the monument and Morality, Law, Education and Freedom are depicted on four buttresses. When the lightning struck the statue about 3 o'clock this morning the Law buttress, weighing more than 50 tons, was pushed back and huge pieces of granite were torn out and thrown more than 300 feet.

Souvenir hunters made raids on the statue today, but the authorities finally collected the pieces and carted them away to a place where they were locked up.

George L. Gooding, who is in charge of the statue, said tonight that no action would be taken on rebuilding it until William Hedge, president of the Pilgrim Society, returns from a trip in the South.

The cornerstone of the statue was laid in 1859 and it was dedicated in 1889. Oliver Ames gave the statue, which was designed by Hammett Billings. The statue was erected by public subscription.

⑨

PILGRIM MONUMENT HIT BY LIGHTNING

Plymouth, Mass., April 4 (P).—The national monument to the pilgrim forefathers, reputedly the largest granite monument in the world, was struck and damaged by lightning during last night's electrical storm. The figure representing Law, near the base of the monument, was badly damaged and the pedestal moved a foot.

⑩

BOYS DAMAGE PILGRIM STATUE

Plymouth Memorial Badly Defaced.

Four Youths, 12 to 14, Accused of Acts of Vandalism.

Large Part Must Be Razed to Make Repairs.

PLYMOUTH, Oct 7—Youthful vandals have so damaged the National memorial to the Forefathers on Monument Hill that it is feared a large part of the structure will have to be razed before the necessary repairs can be made.

Boys,—none of whom is more than 14 years old, disfigured the pedestal of the central figure and the buttresses, and architects report that the damaged stones must be removed.

The monument was struck by lightning on Aug 3. Several large stones at the waist of the heroic figure of Faith, the central one of the group, were displaced. A granite tablet inscribed with the names of the Pilgrims who came over on the Mayflower was blackened by the lightning. The joints on the masonry were sealed with lead and the bolt apparently followed these lines.

It was thought at first that the figure of Faith would have to be taken down and repaired at great expense. A contractor and builder, however, proposed a plan which proved successful and the stones were replaced.

Shortly before the work was completed, it was discovered that some one had damaged the memorial. The work apparently had been done during several nights last week. A watch was set and four boys, between 12 and 14 years of age, were detected committing the acts of vandalism. It was expected that the youths would be compelled to appear in the Juvenile Court.

> "The significance of *Faith, Morality, and Education* not having eyes tells us that they have an inner strength—they bring change from the inside out. On the other hand, *Law* and *Liberty* do have eyes—they are external strengths. When you become a Christian, it brings a change from the inside first—that inward faith then affects your behavior, and brings an outward change. The Pilgrims were Christians. Their inward lives of faith had an external impact on everything they did."
>
> – Leo Martin, Director of Education, The Jenney Interpretive Centeer

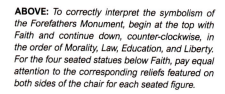

ABOVE: *To correctly interpret the symbolism of the Forefathers Monument, begin at the top with Faith and continue down, counter-clockwise, in the order of Morality, Law, Education, and Liberty. For the four seated statues below Faith, pay equal attention to the corresponding reliefs featured on both sides of the chair for each seated figure.*

INTERPRETING THE MONUMENT

In conceiving his design, architect Hammatt Billings employed artistic imagery to portray "the principles upon which the Pilgrims proposed to found their Commonwealth."[55] Along with various symbolic elements, Billings used the juxtaposition of male and female figures to express the complementary nature of God's creation through internal and external strength. The male figures of *Law* and *Liberty* each have eyes— representing qualities of an outward governance or strength. By contrast, the female figures of *Faith, Morality,* and *Education* do not, which speaks to qualities of inward cultivation and strength.

To correctly interpret the monument, begin at the top and move downward through the seated figures in a counter-clockwise direction. In this manner, it is by *Faith* that we come to know God as revealed in Scripture. God's will for man is expressed in *Morality* and proclaimed through the *Evangelist* and *Prophet*. *Morality* is the foundation for *Law* which is balanced by *Justice* and *Mercy*. Moral laws are perpetuated through *Education* and conveyed by *Wisdom* and *Youth*. *Education* is the final ingredient for *Liberty,* conquering *Tyranny,* and promoting *Peace*. In this depiction of the enduring Pilgrim legacy, each principle lays the foundation for the next—and all are required for freedom to flourish. Remove even one, and *Liberty* fails.

What is hidden under the Monument?

On August 2, 1859, the cornerstone of the Forefathers Monument was set in place. During the ceremony, a time capsule was placed in its foundation. Underneath its 6-ton cornerstone, a small cavity was created to fit a small leaden box approximately five by eleven inches in size. Inside this box, over 30 historical items were sealed into the monument's foundation—including a piece of Plymouth Rock! These items included:

A copy of the 1620 Mayflower Compact; the 1630 Charter for Plymouth colony in New England, granted to William Bradford and his associates; the 1776 Declaration of Independence of the United Colonies of America; the 1787 Constitution of the United States of America; the 1780 Constitution for the Commonwealth of Massachusetts; an 1856 copy of Bradford's History of Plymouth Plantation; an 1846 copy of The Guide to Plymouth, and Recollections of the Pilgrims by William S. Russell; an 1830 Map of the Town of Plymouth; a 1620 Map of Cape Cod Bay, showing the path of the Pilgrims as they sailed from Provincetown Harbor to Plymouth; an 1859 List of Pilgrim Society Officers and Pilgrim Society Membership Diploma; copies of the last weekly issue for the Old Colony Memorial and Plymouth Rock, each being newspapers printed in Plymouth, each containing information about the arrangements for laying the cornerstones of the National Monument, and of the Canopy over Forefathers' Rock; the 1859 Manual for the Use of the General Court of the Commonwealth of Massachusetts; a small portion of Forefathers' Rock; an account of the cornerstone, and Legislative appropriations for alto reliefs; papers, diplomas, certificates, and circulars relating to the monument.

Source: *The Illustrated Pilgrim Memorial, 1863*

MAIN PEDESTAL DEDICATION PANEL:

National Monument to the Forefathers.

Erected by a grateful people in remembrance of their labors, sacrifices and sufferings for the cause of civil and religious liberty.

"Thus, it is our hope that this monument may serve a double purpose. First, let it keep alive in the hearts of later generations the memory of all that our present prosperity has cost; that our ease has been bought with the struggles and privations of many; and that faith and undaunted heroism have entered into the very foundations of our institutions. Let this monument stand, also, as a promise for the future. Let this monument say to him who would honor the Pilgrim, that he can rightfully do so only by practicing the Pilgrim's virtues. May it stand through the years to recall the early days of our country, to the minds of all who behold it, and to bear witness to that surpassing power in the human heart, which reckons pain and suffering of little account, when it is pressing forward to the accomplishment of Divine ends."

Source: Dedication Ceremony for the National Monument to the Forefathers, August 1, 1889, Plymouth, Massachusetts

NATIONAL REGISTER OF HISTORIC PLACES:

The National Monument to the Forefathers was added to the National Register of Historic Places by the National Park Service, the Department of the Interior in September, 1974. The monument, designed by Hammet Billings* of Boston, was erected by the Pilgrim Society in 1889. It possesses exceptional value in commemorating and illustrating the history of the United States.

*An interesting item of note is the misspelling of Hammett Billings' name.

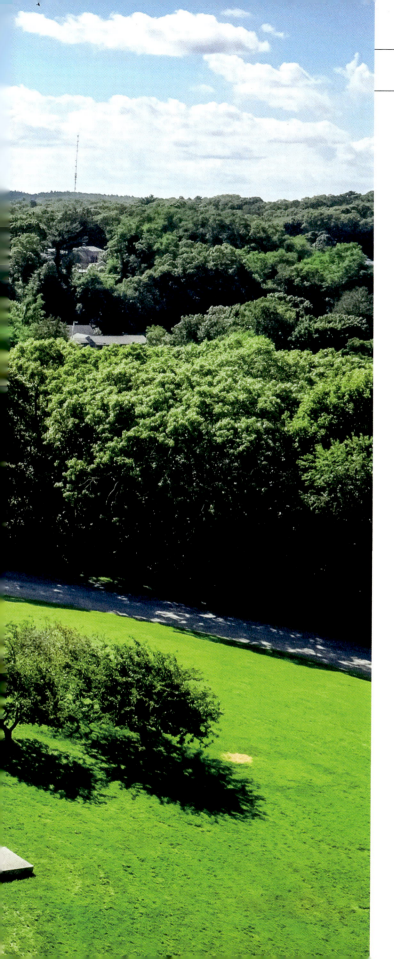

FOREFATHERS MONUMENT GUIDEBOOK

SECTION TWO: SYMBOLISM

"The Pilgrims 'grasped the New Testament notion of spiritual health– Christ-centred faith, hope and love expressed in good works; assurance, peace, and joy; a heart and mind constantly engaged in praise and thanksgiving; and zeal for God's kingdom and glory, leading to purposeful and energetic action.'"

Source: *Puritan Portraits* by J.I. Packer

"Finally, let us not forget the religious character of our origin. Our fathers were brought hither by their high veneration for the Christian religion. They journeyed by its light, and labored in its hope. They sought to incorporate its principles with the elements of their society, and to diffuse its influence through all their institutions, civil, political, or literary."

- Daniel Webster (1782-1852), American constitutional lawyer, statesman, former member of the House of Representatives, Congressman, and U.S. Secretary of State

FAITH

INSTALLED:
August 9, 1877

ORDER:
Faith was the first of the five allegorical figures to be set in place.

COST:
$32,300

SPONSOR:
Hon. Oliver Ames of Easton, Massachusetts

DESIGNER:
Working from the original drawings of Hammatt Billings (1818-74), *Faith* became a collaborative effort by his younger brother, Joseph E. Billings (1821-80), and sculptors John Adams Jackson (1825-79), Joseph Archie, Edward Perry, and William Rimmer (1816-79).

HEIGHT:
36 ft. tall

WEIGHT:
Faith is comprised of 14 blocks of white granite that weigh 180 tons. The granite blocks originally quarried to carve her weighed 400 tons.

PEDESTAL:
45 ft. tall

DIMENSIONS:
Outstretched arms: 10 ft., 1.5 in.
Elbow to fingertip: 9 ft., 9 in.
Forehead circumference: 13 ft., 7 in.
Head to chin: 14 ft., 5 in.
Wrist circumference: 4 ft.
Index finger: 1 ft., 8.5 in.
Neck circumference: 9 ft., 2 in.
Nose length: 1 ft., 4 in.
Star (point to point): 1 ft.

Faith's cubic measurements would yield enough material to carve out 216 life-size granite figures.

ABOVE: *Faith is comprised of 14 white granite blocks that weigh 180 tons.*

As the monument's preeminent figure, *Faith* towers over the seated statues below her as a commanding symbol of the Pilgrim's most defining quality. First and foremost, it was because of their faith in Jesus Christ and their desire to live according to Biblical principles that the Pilgrims "felt called by Scripture and conscience to worship outside the authority of the Church of England—and in their day that was a criminal act under English law."[56]

The Pilgrims were Separatists, a group of Christians who believed that artificial rules and political interference had corrupted England's state-run church beyond all repair. Choosing to leave the Anglican Church rather than compromise their own religious beliefs—these otherwise humble, law-abiding Christians were instantly transformed into criminals and social outcasts.

Hiding out in the English countryside to avoid the authorities, many were exposed by close family members or betrayed by friends. Arrested as traitors and enemies of the state, many Separatists were thrown into London's cold, disease-filled prisons or publicly hanged for their crimes. But despite the overwhelming pressure to comply—to relent and abide by the rules of the church—the Pilgrims refused to back down. Holding fast to their convictions even under threat to their very lives, the Pilgrims were committed to "walk in all His ways… whatever it should cost them, the Lord assisting them."[57]

When England's persecution became more than they could bear, the Pilgrims still refused to abandon their faith—instead, they chose to leave. Lamenting the loss of the only home they had ever known, the Pilgrim's pastor, John Robinson, declared, "Yet for our country, we do not forsake it, but are by it forsaken and expelled by most extreme laws."[58] Several difficult attempts to escape to the nearby Netherlands failed, leaving several Pilgrims jailed and penniless. "For though it was made intolerable for them to stay, they were not allowed to go; the ports were shut against them, so that they had to seek secret means of conveyance, to bribe the captains of ships, and give extraordinary rates for their passages. Often they were betrayed, their goods intercepted, and thereby were put to great trouble and expense."[59] Still, the Pilgrims persevered and eventually succeeded in making their way over to Holland.

Settling in the cosmopolitan city of Leiden, the Pilgrims were finally free to gather and worship openly as a church—and "be ruled by the laws of God's word."[60] Armed with faith and patience, they worked diligently to make a new life for themselves in a foreign land and culture. "They fell to such trades and employments as they best could, valuing peace and their spiritual comfort above any other riches whatever; and at length they came to raise a competent and comfortable living, though only by dint of hard and continual labour."[61]

Unfettered by the constant threats of persecution that dogged them in England, the Pilgrims enjoyed deep fellowship as a congregation in Leiden. "Their desires were set on the ways of God, to enjoy His ordinances; they rested on His providence, and knew Whom they had believed."[62] Bradford wrote about these early years together in Leiden as a church, and how the congregation "grew in knowledge and other gifts and graces of the spirit of God, and lived together in peace and love and holiness… and if any differences arose or offences broke out, as cannot but be even amongst the best of men, they were always so met with and nipped in the head… that love, peace, and communion continued."[63]

ABOVE: *In a scene similar to how the Pilgrims left Holland, Dutch artist Willem van de Velde the Younger paints a vessel-filled harbor.*

"Therefore, as God's chosen people, holy and dearly loved, clothe yourselves with compassion, kindness, humility, gentleness and patience. Bear with each other and forgive one another if any of you has a grievance against someone. Forgive as the Lord forgave you. And over all these virtues put on love, which binds them all together in perfect unity. Let the peace of Christ rule in your hearts, since as members of one body you were called to peace. And be thankful. Let the message of Christ dwell among you richly as you teach and admonish one another with all wisdom through psalms, hymns, and songs from the Spirit, singing to God with gratitude in your hearts. And whatever you do, whether in word or deed, do it all in the name of the Lord Jesus, giving thanks to God the Father through him." - Colossians 3:12-17

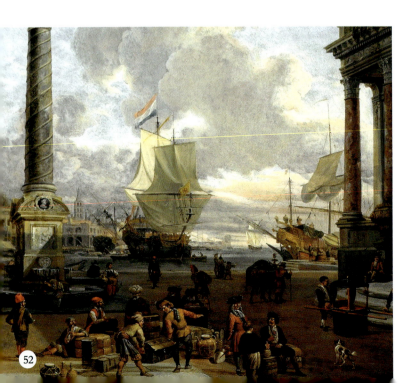

But this freedom came at a price. After a decade of living together as a church in Holland, the heavy physical labor, worldly Dutch culture, and the fading influence of their English heritage took their toll on the congregation. The Pilgrims agonized about how to preserve their faith and culture for future generations. Failing that, every sacrifice they had made up to that point would be in vain.

The decision was made to leave. For those who first set sail for America, there was no way to know what dangers might lie ahead—or if they would even survive the journey across the Atlantic Ocean. Others had attempted it before them, often with disastrous results. But despite the risks, the Pilgrims determined to forge ahead in faith, believing that "all of them, through the help of God, by fortitude and patience, might either be borne or overcome."[64]

LEFT: *A typical 17th-century Dutch harbor by Dutch artist Abraham Storck.*

"In several of these storms the wind was so strong and the seas so high that they could not carry a knot of sail." - William Bradford

ABOVE: In "Ships on a Stormy Sea," artist Raden Saleh painted the tumultuous waves of a storm-tossed ocean, a common occurrence for the Mayflower during her voyage at sea.

> Despite unimaginable trials and unspeakable grief, the Pilgrims never gave into bitterness— instead, they credited God for their deliverance.
>
> By spring, when most of their sick had finally recovered, Bradford reflected that they had "borne their sad afflictions with as much patience and contentedness as I think any people could do. But it was the Lord who upheld them."

Delayed by repairs and blown off course for days on end—when the *Mayflower* finally reached Plymouth harbor, winter was bearing down quickly, and the ship's bow cut through icy water. By then, the Pilgrims had endured two months at sea confined below deck in cramped, foul-smelling quarters as the *Mayflower* lurched and heaved through violent storms. When they finally reached land, the Pilgrims were cold, tired, and malnourished from the arduous journey. Going ashore to build shelters in frigid weather, it wasn't long before many became deathly ill. But even in their darkest moments of distress—often with two and three people dying in a single day—the Pilgrims expressed their faith in practical ways, knowing that "faith by itself, if it is not accompanied by action, is dead." (James 2:17) Selflessly caring for the sick, they showed no partiality in serving beloved friends and strangers alike.

Bradford writes: "There were but six or seven sound persons, who, to their great commendation be it spoken, spared no pains night or day, but with great toil and at the risk of their own health, fetched wood, made fires, prepared food for the sick, made their beds, washed their infected clothes, dressed and undressed them… all this they did willingly and cheerfully, without the least grudging, showing their love to the friends and brethren; a rare example, and worthy to be remembered… while they had health or strength, they forsook none that had need of them. I doubt not that their recompense is with the Lord."[65] Despite unimaginable trials and grief, the Pilgrims never gave in to bitterness. Instead, they credited God for their deliverance. By spring, when most of their sick had finally recovered, Bradford reflected that they had "borne their sad afflictions with as much patience and contentedness as I think any people could do. But it was the Lord who upheld them."[66]

From the filthy jails of London to the sweat-filled factories in Leiden, to the bitterly cold shores of Cape Cod—at each pivotal moment of the Pilgrim story, these extraordinary men and women were determined to live—*and even die, if the Lord allowed it*—according to the convictions of their faith. As the culmination of their spiritual journey, the Pilgrims were convinced God had led them to plant a new settlement at Plymouth Colony. With unshakeable faith, they believed that from these humble beginnings—one small candle could light a thousand, and the light of the Gospel could reach an entire nation.

In the spring of 1621, when the *Mayflower* sailed out of Plymouth harbor to begin her return voyage back to England, not a single Pilgrim was onboard. Despite the astonishing offer of free passage from Captain Jones to anyone in the settlement who wanted to leave, "All of them—every survivor, men and women alike—had opted to remain at their new home: Plymouth Colony. Whatever awaited them in the future, they had chosen to face it in America."[67]

> From the filthy jails of London, to the sweat-filled factories in Leiden, to the bitterly cold shores of Cape Cod—at each pivotal moment of the Pilgrim story, these extraordinary men and women were determined to live—*and even die, if the Lord allowed it*—according to the convictions of their faith.

POINTING TO HEAVEN

As the monument's predominant figure, *Faith* is shown pointing her audience toward heaven and the presence of God. In this depiction, *Faith* is revealed as the key to encountering God, for "without faith it is impossible to please God, because anyone who comes to him must believe that he exists and that he rewards those who earnestly seek him." (Hebrews 11:6) The Pilgrims pored over stories in Scripture that demonstrated God's redemptive works on earth. They believed that salvation could only be found through faith in Jesus Christ, "for there is no other name under heaven given to mankind by which we must be saved." (Acts 4:12)

"If no place upon the face of the earth should be free for us... we have a most assured hope, that heaven itself is open for us by Christ, who is the way."
- William Bradford

The term "pilgrim" was first recorded by William Bradford in his journals. Writing about their decision to leave Leiden for a new start in America, he explained: "So they left that good and pleasant city, which had been their resting place for nearly twelve years; but they knew they were pilgrims, and lifted up their eyes to the heavens, their dearest country, and quieted their spirits."[68] Although the Pilgrims were happy and optimistic by nature and fully embraced life—Bradford's words capture the longings of a people who knew they were destined for a different world. The Pilgrims believed their true citizenship—and ultimate home—was with God in heaven, which filled them with hope. Even as they yearned to be free on earth, they were confident that "if no place upon the face of the earth should be free for us… we have a most assured hope, that heaven itself is open for us by Christ, who is the way."[69]

CROWNED WITH A STAR

Faith is crowned with a prominent star on her head, a symbol used throughout Scripture to indicate Divine guidance or leadership. In one of the most well-known examples, the book of Matthew recounts the story of the Magi, or wise men from the east, who followed a bright star to Bethlehem to worship and present gifts to the infant Jesus, the newborn King. "After they had heard the king, they went on their way, and the star they had seen when it rose went ahead of them until it stopped over the place where the child was." (Matthew 2:9) Here, *Faith* is depicted as a Divine messenger pointing her audience to the presence of God in heaven.

HOLDING A BIBLE

Faith holds a Geneva Bible in her left hand, which was first brought to America by the Pilgrims on the *Mayflower*. For centuries in the early church, the Bible's meaning was obscured in ancient languages—and a priest would translate the text of Scripture from Latin into English for the congregation. Actual copies of the Bible were rare; many were chained to a church's pulpit. But with the advent of the printing press, all of that changed. Bibles were translated into English and became widely available—allowing everyone to read and study God's word for themselves. The Pilgrims were heavily influenced by early Reformers such as Martin Luther, who argued that "any believer should be allowed to read the Bible without the oversight of a minister or priest."[70] As Christians, the Pilgrims embraced the Bible as God's eternal truth and searched the Scriptures daily for instruction, encouragement, and revelation.

> The English philosopher Francis Bacon, who's credited with developing the scientific method, wrote in 1620 that the three inventions that forever changed the world were gunpowder, the nautical compass and the printing press.
>
> Source: *7 Ways The Printing Press Changed The World* by Dave Roos

Unique in church history, the Geneva Bible is often referred to as the world's first study Bible. It was written in common, everyday English for easy comprehension and featured a clear, Roman-style typeface, which made the text comfortable to read. It was the first Bible to include numbered chapters and verses and featured scriptural cross-references for deeper study. Its margins were filled with notes and commentary from prominent Reformers like John Calvin, which helped explain more complex passages to the average reader. The Geneva Bible also included maps, illustrations, indexes, charts, and a lexicon of Biblical words and terms. Although such Bible study aids are common today—they were revolutionary for early Christians in that era. The Geneva Bible was a treasured possession of every Pilgrim family, and today, Governor Bradford's own Geneva Bible is on display at the Pilgrim Hall Museum in Plymouth, Massachusetts.

TOP RIGHT: *Babworth's Church in Nottinghamshire, where Separatist Pastor Richard Clyfton served from 1586-1604, and a teenaged William Bradford attended worship services before joining the church at Scrooby. Much of the building dates from the 15th century, and the stone church is approximately 900 years old.* **MIDDLE:** *The church displays 19th-century-stained glass by Victorian designer Charles Eamer Kempe (1837-1907) that pays tribute to Bradford's baptism and the Mayflower Compact.* **BOTTOM:** *The church contains several rare Pilgrim artifacts, including a 1605 Bible and silver chalice used by Pastor Clyfton for communion services. The silver hallmark on the chalice dates back to the late 16th century, which means Bradford almost certainly used it to take communion as a new believer. To learn more about this unique region in early Pilgrim history, visit the "Pilgrims Gallery" at Bassetlaw Museum at: www.pilgrimroots.co.uk*

THE HISTORY OF PLYMOUTH ROCK

Source: *History of the Town of Plymouth, From its First Settlement in 1620 to the Present Time* by James Thatcher

> The fact of its identity has been transmitted from father to son, particularly in the instance of Elder Faunce and his father, as would be the richest inheritance, by unquestionable tradition. About the year 1741, it was represented to Elder Faunce that a wharf was to be erected over the rock, which impressed his mind with deep concern, and excited a strong desire to take a last farewell of the cherished object. He was then ninety-five years old, and resided three miles from the place. A chair was procured, and the venerable man conveyed to the shore, where a number of the inhabitants were assembled to witness the patriarch's benediction. Having pointed out the rock directly under the bank of Cole's Hill, which his father had assured him was that, which had received the footsteps of our fathers on their first arrival, and which should be perpetuated to posterity, he bedewed it with his tears and bid to it an everlasting adieu. These facts were testified to by the late venerable Deacon Spooner, who was then a boy and was present on the interesting occasion. Tradition says that Elder Faunce was in the habit on every anniversary, of placing his children and grand-children on the rock, and conversing with them respecting their forefathers.

ABOVE: *An early view from the monument's grounds reveal the original ocean view, with the faint image of the Myles Standish Monument in Duxbury visible in the distance.*

WHO WAS THOMAS FAUNCE?

Thomas Faunce had close ties to the Pilgrims who came to Plymouth in 1620. In 1623, at age 15, Thomas' father, John, sailed to Plymouth on board the Anne. He was part of the initial group known as "firstcomers" in the colony, and the Faunce family was extremely close to the Bradfords. Thomas was just seven years old when his father, John, died in 1653 at the age of 47, and young Thomas grew up surrounded by his father's friends and contemporaries. To put his life experiences in perspective, Thomas was nine years old when Myles Standish died, and he was 11 years old when Governor William Bradford passed away at 63. When Bradford's wife Alice died in 1670, a 23-year-old Thomas gave her eulogy at her memorial service. Thomas was 26 years old when John Howland died, and he was 40 years old when John Alden was buried. Incredibly, 23 of the original Pilgrims were still alive during most of his youth. Thomas served as a deacon of the First Church in 1686 and as an elder in 1694. He was selected to serve as the first clerk by Plymouth and Plympton Commons proprietors, where he played an integral role in keeping the official records for Plymouth. At the age of 95 and close to death, Thomas asked to be carried down to the waterfront to bid a tearful goodbye to the rock which held the first steps of the Pilgrim's arrival in the new colony at Plymouth.

Source: *Thomas Faunce: The Man Who Saved Plymouth Rock* by Dr. Paul Jehle, Plymouth Rock Foundation

In a final element of symbolism, the pages of *Faith's* Geneva Bible can be seen fluttering open at the top—a purposeful detail. Throughout the Bible, God's full nature is revealed in the three distinct personalities of the Godhead: God the Father, God the Son, and God the Holy Spirit—commonly referred to as the Trinity. The Pilgrims believed "all Scripture is God-breathed and is useful for teaching, rebuking, correcting and training in righteousness." (2 Timothy 3:16) Here, the pages of *Faith's* Bible have been blown open by the Holy Spirit, "For the word of God is alive and active. Sharper than any double-edged sword, it penetrates even to dividing soul and spirit, joints and marrow; it judges the thoughts and attitudes of the heart." (Hebrews 4:12) The Pilgrims left the Church of England when it exalted human tradition over the authority of Holy Scripture, and they risked their lives to live and worship God according to the Bible.

FOOT UPON PLYMOUTH ROCK

Facing east, where the Pilgrims first began their journey, *Faith* stands with her foot planted on Plymouth Rock—the historic site where the Pilgrims first came ashore at Plymouth. Now enshrined on the Plymouth waterfront, Plymouth Rock has come to symbolize freedom for many Americans and represents the humble beginnings of a new nation. The Pilgrims' first steps onto Plymouth Rock were the answer to many "humble prayers to God for His protection and assistance" in their journey to build a colony in the new world.[71] And throughout their story, in one surprising twist after the next—God appears to intervene for these exact reasons.

A GREAT IRON SCREW

In William Bradford's journals, which were collected and published in the best-selling book, *Of Plymouth Plantation,* he chronicled the fierce storms they encountered while at sea. One storm in particular pounded the *Mayflower* with such force that it caused a catastrophic break in the ship's main beam—a fatal event. As the crew rushed to hold the beam in place and prevent its complete collapse, a "great iron screw" was miraculously discovered. Twisting this large screw into place under the beam, the crew was able to secure the broken beam and save the ship.

A large iron screw such as this is not typically found on a sailing vessel, and Bradford never explained where it came from. Some speculate that it came from a makeshift printing press back in Leiden. Others believe it came from building jacks that were brought to build homes in the new colony. Regardless of why it was on the ship, there is no doubt that without this unusual item onboard—the *Mayflower* would have certainly been lost at sea. Once her main beam was secured, the *Mayflower* held fast through several other storms that eventually pushed the ship hundreds of miles off course.

ABOVE: *In his work, "The Seas Were So High," marine artist Mike Haywood paints the tempestuous Atlantic route of the Mayflower. In his journals, Bradford wrote of storms so fierce that the crew was forced to drop sails and drift until violent weather subsided.*

PLYMOUTH BAY

When the Pilgrims first sighted land, it was not at the mouth of the Hudson River as expected—but far north in the waters of Cape Cod. As they continued sailing down the tip of the Cape toward Virginia, the weather took a swift and frightening turn. "Before they could change course, the Mayflower sailed into dangerous shoals, roaring surf, and boiling seas. Terrified, many of the passengers huddled together anticipating the ship to run aground or capsize."[72] Bradford explained their decision to turn back, writing: "They conceived themselves in great danger—the wind falling—they resolved to bear up again for the Cape… and by God's providence they… found a good haven… and they fell upon their knees and blessed the God of Heaven who had brought them over the vast and furious ocean… to set their feet upon the firm and stable earth."[73] After 66 grueling days on the open sea, the Pilgrims finally reached land—albeit not the land they had intended. Treacherous conditions forced the *Mayflower* to abandon her southern course to Virginia, and many believed Divine Providence had guided them into the safe harbor of what came to be known as Plymouth Bay. But would the Pilgrims be able to survive in the wilderness?

PLAGUES AND PROVISION

When the *Mayflower* finally reached land, its passengers had spent over nine weeks at sea. They were weak, hungry, and dangerously low on supplies. A small team was dispatched to take the shallop to scout the coastline and explore the land on foot. Arriving in Nauset, the Pilgrims discovered an abandoned village that seemed deserted for the winter—or so they thought.

ABOVE: *The Pilgrim's shallop is seen in "Mayflower in Plymouth Harbor" by English artist William Halsall (1841-1919), who lived in Provincetown, Massachusetts, and later became a U.S. citizen.*

They later learned that a coastal plague had struck the region in 1616, killing off 95 percent of the Wampanoag tribe over three devastating years. Because of this, the entire area was considered cursed by the natives. Had the Pilgrims arrived any sooner than 1620—there is little doubt that they too would have fallen victim to this deadly plague. However, walking through an empty village that day, the Pilgrims were oblivious to the terrible fate of its former occupants. What they found instead was a hidden stash of corn.

According to Bradford, "These they brought away, intending to give them full satisfaction when they should meet with any of them—as about six months afterwards they did. And it is… a special providence of God… that they thus got seed to plant corn the next year, or they might have starved; for they had none, nor any likelihood of getting any, till too late for the planting season."[74] Desperate for food, the Pilgrims believed that Divine Providence had guided them to these hidden reserves of corn—but even so, seeds alone were no guarantee. In such harsh wilderness conditions, how could they successfully cultivate any crops?

ABOVE: *Moored in Plymouth harbor, the "Shallop Elizabeth Tilley" is a 38-foot, 7-ton wooden replica of the boat used by the Pilgrims. The shallop is visible from land by Plymouth Rock, and owned by the Pilgrim John Howland Society. www.pilgrimjohnhowlandsociety.org*

"So they committed themselves to the will of God, and resolved to proceed."

- William Bradford

A SPECIAL INSTRUMENT OF GOD

The Pilgrims' first encounters with the Indians had turned violent. These early skirmishes only added to their shock when "about the 16th of March a certain Indian came boldly among them, and spoke to them in broken English, which they could well understand, but were astonished at it. His name was Samoset; he told them also of another Indian, whose name was Squanto, a native of this part, who had been in England and could speak English better than himself."[75] Several days later, Samoset returned and introduced the Pilgrims to Squanto, also known as Tisquantum, a member of the Patuxet tribe. Squanto became an invaluable friend to the Pilgrims, a man Bradford later described as "a special instrument sent of God for their good."[76]

Meeting a native who spoke fluent English was remarkable, but Squanto gained his language skills through a series of tragic events. Kidnapped as a young boy and taken to London, Squanto lived there for years before trying to get back home—only to be kidnapped again. When Spanish monks miraculously liberated his slave ship, Squanto returned to England and lived with a merchant's family for several years. When he was finally able to return home to his village at Patuxet, Squanto found it empty. The coastal plague of 1616 wiped out his entire tribe and family. Alone and despondent, Squanto lived in solitude before approaching Chief Massasoit, the grand sachem of the Wampanoag Indian tribes. Seeing the value of Squanto's upbringing and language skills, Massasoit took him in.

ABOVE: *In late July of 1621, six-year-old John Billington wandered away from Plymouth colony and became lost. A search party was sent to find him, and Squanto was instrumental in bringing him safely home. In an illustration from a 1922 children's storybook, Squanto carries a young John safely on his shoulders back to the colony.*

As a translator, Squanto was crucial in facilitating the peace agreement between the Pilgrims and Chief Massasoit. After the peace treaty was signed, Squanto stayed with the Pilgrims in his boyhood village of Patuxet—later known as Plymouth colony. While living in his old village with the Pilgrims, Squanto proved indispensable to the struggling colonists. He taught them to catch eels in streams and trap fish using dams. He showed them how to fertilize their crops using dead fish, a technique that would help the Pilgrims cultivate over twenty acres for harvest. Squanto became a friend to the entire colony but was incredibly close to Governor Bradford. When he fell deathly ill the following year, he sought comfort in his dear friend. "Before he died, Squanto asked Bradford to pray for him so that 'he might go to the Englishmen's God in Heaven.' He also bequeathed his few belongings to his English friends so that they might remember him. His death, Bradford wrote, was a 'great loss' to the entire colony. In all likelihood, Bradford felt a mixture of sorrow at the death of his friend, without whom the Pilgrims would have perished in the wilderness, and joy that Squanto had converted to Christianity before his death."[77]

BELOW: *An early winter's snowfall at Plymouth harbor reveals the same icy conditions the Pilgrims encountered when they came ashore to build shelters on land.*

The entire Pilgrim story is a stream of improbable yet pivotal events. While at sea, the *Mayflower* averted a near-certain disaster with the unlikely discovery of a giant iron screw, which enabled the crew to secure the ship's main beam. On Cape Cod, when treacherous waves forced the *Mayflower* to turn around and sail north to safety, the Pilgrims discovered an ideal harbor location for their new colony. Desperate for food, the Pilgrims found a stash of corn in a village deserted by its inhabitants due to a deadly plague they had avoided by mere *months*. And somehow, of all the native Indian tribes scattered along the east coast, the Pilgrims crossed paths with one who spoke perfect English. Their unlikely friendship with Squanto helped them broker peace with other tribes and taught them the necessary skills to survive in the wilderness.

For the Pilgrims, these astonishing events were proof of Divine Providence—and provided compelling evidence of God's direct intervention in their lives. Every instance of miraculous timing or provision was a resounding answer to Bradford's question: "What, then, could now sustain them but the spirit of God, and His grace?"[18]

"We have no government armed with power capable of contending with human passions unbridled by morality and religion… our Constitution was made only for a moral and religious people. It is wholly inadequate to the government of any other."

- John Adams (1735-1826), American Founding Father, signer of the *Declaration of Independence* (1776), author of the *Massachusetts Constitution* (1780), and second President of the United States (1797-1801)

MORALITY

ABOVE: *Morality was the first statue to be placed after Faith was installed.*

INSTALLED:
August 5, 1878

ORDER:
Morality was the second of the five allegorical figures to be set in place.

COST:
$10,000

SPONSOR:
Massachusetts Legislature

DESIGNER:
Working from the original drawings of Hammatt Billings (1818-74), *Morality* was modeled by Carl Conrads (b.1839).

HEIGHT:
14 ft., 6 in. tall

WEIGHT:
Morality weighs approximately 25 tons, cut from a single block.

DIMENSIONS:
Head circumference (at the forehead): 7 ft.

Top of the head to the bottom of the chin: 2 ft.

LOWER MARBLE BAS-RELIEF PANEL:
Embarkation was modeled by Carl Conrads (b.1839), and its cost of $3,000 was sponsored by the Connecticut Legislature.

As the first of the seated statues in the gallery below *Faith, Morality* represents a vital component of the Pilgrim legacy—and a fundamental requirement for self-government. In 1798, President John Adams, noted signer of the *Declaration of Independence* and *Bill of Rights,* said of America: "We have no government armed with power capable of contending with human passions unbridled by morality and religion… our Constitution was made only for a moral and religious people. It is wholly inadequate to the government of any other."[79]

For the Pilgrims, morality was more than simply a set of rules to follow—it also embodied the moral character and ethics displayed in everyday life. By every reliable account, the Pilgrims were characterized as honest, hard-working, charitable, and kind. Despite their diverse English backgrounds, the congregation lived peacefully together in "love and holiness" as a church in Leiden. "And if any differences arose or offences broke out—as cannot but be even amongst the best of men—they were always so met with and nipped in the head… that love, peace, and communion continued."[80]

As immigrants in Holland, the Pilgrims were also highly regarded in their local communities. Although the Pilgrims were considered poor, the Dutch business owners came to know their character and extended them credit. Shopkeepers and bakers "would trust them to any reasonable extent when they lacked money to buy what they needed. They found by experience how careful they were to keep their word, and saw how diligent they were."[81] In Leiden, the Dutch merchants competed heartily for the Pilgrim's business. When hiring staff, they often employed Pilgrims in preference over others.

The Pilgrims believed it was their duty to model the Christian virtues revealed in the Bible and taught in church. Pastor Robinson taught emphatically against religious hypocrites—those who claimed to love God but failed to love their neighbor. He admonished that any display of devotion to God in church, should be equally matched "in the house, and streets, with loving-kindness, and mercy and all goodness towards men."[82] The Biblical command to "do to others as you would have them do to you" (Luke 6:31), later known as the *Golden Rule,* would be evident throughout the Pilgrim story, even to those who ridiculed their faith.

ABOVE: *Morality cradles the Decalogue, which displays the first two of the Ten Commandments given to Moses in the Old Testament (see right.)*

TEN COMMANDMENTS

In her left-hand, *Morality* holds the Decalogue, more commonly known as the *Ten Commandments*, which were the written laws given to Moses in the Old Testament. The book of Deuteronomy recounts how Moses received these commandments from God Himself at the top of Mount Sinai: "These are the commandments the Lord proclaimed in a loud voice to your whole assembly there on the mountain from out of the fire, the cloud and the deep darkness; and he added nothing more. Then he wrote them on two stone tablets and gave them to me." (Deuteronomy 5:22)

LAW OF NATURE

The Ten Commandments express a principle known as the *Law of Nature*, a term also used in the *Declaration of Independence*. Simply put, the *Law of Nature* is the understanding that God has implanted morality—or intrinsic sense of right from wrong—inside each person's heart in the form of a conscience. The Apostle Paul affirmed this, writing, "Indeed, when Gentiles, who do not have the law, do by nature things required by the law… they show that the requirements of the law are written on their hearts, their consciences also bearing witness, and their thoughts sometimes accusing them and at other times even defending them." (Romans 2:14-15) The Pilgrims believed the *Law of Nature*— each person's conscience or innate understanding of right and wrong— received its full expression in the *Moral Law* found in Scripture.

Noah Webster (1758-1843), the famous textbook pioneer, lexicographer, and considered the "Father of American Scholarship and Education," explained how the Bible reveals the moral laws of God: "The duties of men are summarily comprised in the Ten Commandments, consisting of two tables. One, comprehending the duties which we owe immediately to God—the other, the duties we owe to our fellow men. Christ himself has reduced these commandments under two general precepts, which enjoin upon us, to love the Lord our God with all our heart, with all our soul, with all our mind and with all our strength—and to love our neighbor as ourselves. On these two commandments hang all the law and the prophets—that is, they comprehend the substance of all the doctrines and precepts of the Bible, or the whole of religion."[83]

> " For since the creation of the world God's invisible qualities—his eternal power and divine nature—have been clearly seen, being understood from what has been made, so that people are without excuse.
> (Romans 1:20) "

God spoke these words saying,
I am the Lord your God:

I.
You shall have no other gods before Me.
II.
You shall make no idols.
III.
You shall not take the name of the Lord your God in vain.
IV.
Keep the Sabbath day holy.
V.
Honor your father and mother.
VI.
You shall not murder.
VII.
You shall not commit adultery.
VIII.
You shall not steal.
IX.
You shall not bear false witness against your neighbor.
X.
You shall not covet.

BELOW: *Moses, returning from Mount Sinai with the Ten Commandments, is depicted in stained glass.*

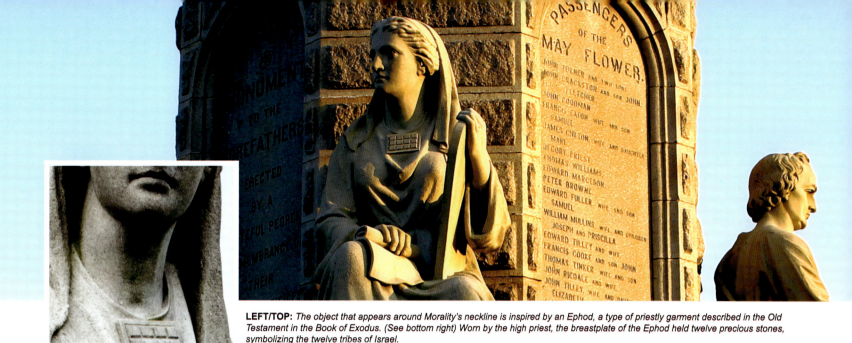

LEFT/TOP: The object that appears around Morality's neckline is inspired by an Ephod, a type of priestly garment described in the Old Testament in the Book of Exodus. (See bottom right) Worn by the high priest, the breastplate of the Ephod held twelve precious stones, symbolizing the twelve tribes of Israel.

As Christians, the Pilgrims were guided by the *Law of Nature,* their conscience, fulfilled in God's *Moral Law* as revealed in Holy Scripture. They were eager to build a God-honoring settlement at Plymouth and "establish a culture in the wilderness that would be free from the corruptions of the Old World. The Bible was the 'perfect rule of faith,' the daily source of moral guidance and spiritual support."[84]

REVELATION SCROLL

In her right-hand, *Morality* holds the scroll of Revelation to represent the final book in Scripture. Derived from the Greek word *apokalypsis*, the word "revelation" translates as "uncovering" or "unveiling" to describe a series of visions the Apostle John received while exiled on the Greek island of Patmos. Often symbolic, the book of Revelation is the only book in Scripture where Jesus speaks directly to the reader as the incarnate Christ, saying: "Behold, I am coming soon, and My reward is with Me, to give to each one according to what he has done. I am the Alpha and the Omega, the First and the Last, the Beginning and the End." (Rev. 22:12-13) For those who reject the saving work of Jesus Christ, the book of Revelation holds a somber preview of coming judgment. For Christ's faithful followers, it reveals the fullness of God's redemptive plan for His creation—along with the promise of eternal fellowship and reward. The Pilgrims held fast to these promises and looked forward to "a glorious resurrection, knowing Christ Jesus after the flesh no more; but, looking unto the joy that is before us, we will endure all these things and account them light in comparison of the joy we hope for."[85]

PRIESTLY GARMENT

On her chest, *Morality* is wearing a decorative panel that mimics the breastplate of an Ephod, a type of priestly garment described in the Book of Exodus. The Pilgrims were part of the Protestant Reformation, which held the core doctrine of a "priesthood of all believers." As Christians, they believed "all humans have access to God through Christ, the true high priest, and thus do not need a priestly mediator. This introduced a democratic element in the functioning of the church that meant all Christians were equal."[86] This priestly element associated with *Morality* highlights the Pilgrim's unique spiritual identity as God's "chosen people, a royal priesthood, a holy nation, (and) God's special possession." (1 Peter 2:9)

ABOVE: The Kohen Gadol (High Priest of Israel) is shown wearing an Ephod, the priestly vestments described in Exodus 28.

THE EVANGELIST

On the right side of *Morality's* pedestal is the *Evangelist,* or someone who shares the gospel or "good news" of salvation through Jesus Christ. In the New Testament, Jesus issued the *Great Commission* to his followers when He told them: "Go therefore and make disciples of all nations, baptizing them in the name of the Father and of the Son and of the Holy Spirit, teaching them to observe all that I have commanded you. And behold, I am with you always, to the end of the age." (Matthew 28:19-20) Here, the *Evangelist* is shown with a quill pen and an open book, poised to record the names of new believers in the *Book of Life*.

BOOK OF LIFE

In the Bible, many scriptures reference a Divine book that records the names of those who have received eternal life. In the Old Testament, the Psalmist refers to a *"book of life."* In the New Testament, the Apostle Paul addresses his co-laborers in ministry as those *"whose names are in the book of life."* In the final book of Revelation, the Apostle John describes heaven as a place reserved for those whose names *"are written in the Lamb's book of life."* By holding the Book of Life in his hands, the *Evangelist* signals the Pilgrim's earnest desire to spread the gospel to untouched parts of the world.

Indeed, when Bradford chronicled the church's decision to leave Holland for a new start in America, he wrote:

> *"Last and not least, they cherished a great hope and inward zeal of laying good foundations, or at least of making some way towards it, for the propagation and advance of the gospel of the kingdom of Christ in the remote parts of the world, even though they should be but stepping stones to others in the performance of so great a work."* [87]

"*The question… has been asked before, how it happened, that a company of wanderers, without military force and with little wealth… could endure such trials… and this question finds its answer in the religious character of the Colony.*

Worldly objects were with them secondary, and political ambition found no place among them. Religious faith enabled them to do and endure, under a sense of duty, and for the sake of God and humanity, what no mere selfish purpose was ever yet able to accomplish.

They were men that feared God, and could lay down their lives for a principle; and so they lived and 'died in faith, not having received the promises, but having seen them afar off, and were persuaded of them, and embraced them, and confessed that they were strangers and pilgrims on the earth.'"

Source: *The Pilgrim Fathers: A Glance At Their History, Character And Principles, In Two Memorial Discourses, Delivered In The First Congregational Church, Rockford, May 22, 1870* by Henry Martyn Goodwin

"We have staked the whole future of American civilization, not upon the power of government, far from it. We have staked the future of all of our political institutions… upon the capacity of each and all of us to govern ourselves… according to the Ten Commandments of God."

- James Madison (1751-1836), American statesman, Founding Father, and fourth President of the United States

THE PROPHET

On the left side of *Morality's* pedestal is the *Prophet,* someone who speaks a message on behalf of God. Here, the *Prophet* is portrayed as Moses on Mount Sinai—as he holds the stone tablets of the Decalogue and lifts his hand toward the face of God. In the Old Testament, the prophet Amos declared, "Surely the Sovereign Lord does nothing without revealing his plan to his servants the prophets" (Amos 3:7), and Scripture is filled with instances where God chose unlikely people to fulfill His plans. Before He brought judgment in the form of a flood, God chose Noah to rescue a remnant of His creation. Before He delivered the Israelites out of slavery in Egypt, God chose Moses to be a leader for his people. When Jesus began his public ministry, He chose twelve ordinary men to spread the gospel and declared—"upon this rock I will build my church; and the gates of hell shall not prevail against it." (Matthew 16:18)

ABOVE: *In 1878, a completed Morality sits in the quarry yard, awaiting final transport to Plymouth.*

The Pilgrims were inspired by these stories of how God used ordinary, even flawed people to accomplish His plans on earth—and prayed they could also be used for Divine ends. "More than 150 years passed before the descendants of New England's founders finally united with the other English colonists to challenge an empire and achieve independence. The passage of five generations meant profound changes in wealth, values, occupations, communication, political philosophy, and even theology among the thriving providences of eighteenth-century English America. But one characteristic consistently connected the Pilgrims of 1620 and the patriots of 1776: an unshakable conviction in their own significance as part of a divinely ordained design for their country."[88]

> What is liberty without wisdom and without virtue? It is the greatest of all possible evils; for it is folly, vice, and madness, without restraint. Men are qualified for civil liberty in exact proportion to their disposition to put moral chains upon their own appetites... society cannot exist, unless a controlling power upon *will* and *appetite* be placed somewhere; and the less of it there is within, the more there must be without. It is ordained in the eternal constitution of things, that men of intemperate minds cannot be free. Their passions forge their fetters.
>
> - Edmund Burke (1729-1797), Irish statesman, economist, philosopher and member of parliament in the House of Commons of Great Britain (1766, 1794)

MARBLE BAS-RELIEF PANEL: THE EMBARKATION

On July 22, 1620, the Pilgrims left the port city of Delftshaven onboard the *Speedwell*—bound for Southhampton, England, where they would join the rest of their waiting party on the *Mayflower*. William Bradford recorded the poignant scene of their morning departure as the Pilgrims left for a new start in America. For many that day, it would be the last time they saw their loved ones.

"When they came to the place, they found the ship and everything ready, and such of their friends as could not come with them followed them, and several came from Amsterdam to see them shipped and to take leave of them. That night there was little sleep for most of them, for it was spent in friendly entertainment and Christian discourse and other real expressions of true Christian love. The next day the wind being fair they went aboard and their friends with them—and truly doleful was the sight of that sad and mournful parting. What sighs and sobs and prayers rose from amongst them! What tears gushed from every eye, and pithy speeches pierced each heart! Many of the Dutch strangers who stood on the quay as spectators, could not refrain from tears. Yet it was comfortable and sweet to see such lively and true expressions of dear and unfeigned love. But the tide which stays for no man called them away, though loth to part; and their reverent pastor, falling down on his knees, and all with him, with watery cheeks commended them with most fervent prayers to the Lord and His blessing. Then with mutual embraces and many tears, they took their leave of one another—which proved to be the last leave for many of them."[89]

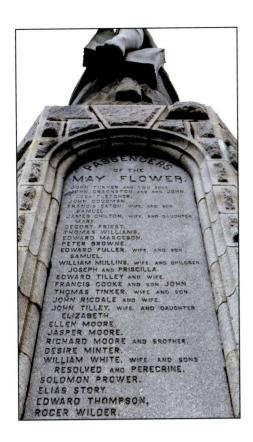

PANEL: PASSENGERS OF THE MAYFLOWER

Although the Pilgrims knew the journey to America was dangerous, they proceeded with clear-eyed optimism and courage. After nine perilous weeks at sea, the *Mayflower* finally reached land—but delays and detours had pushed them to the brink of winter, and "the ground was soon all covered with snow and frozen hard."[90] Weary and malnourished, many became gravely ill. Entire families were wiped out in what became known as *"The Great Sickness."* Elder William Brewster and Captain Myles Standish were among the few that were healthy enough to help care for the sick, and William Bradford memorialized their heroic efforts in his journal.

"In the time of worst distress, there were but six or seven sound persons, who, to their great commendation be it spoken, spared no pains night or day, but with great toil and at the risk of their own health, fetched wood, made fires, prepared food for the sick, made their beds, washed their infected clothes, dressed and undressed them; in a word did all the homely and necessary services for them which dainty and queasy stomachs cannot endure to hear mentioned; all this they did willingly and cheerfully, without the least grudging, showing their love to the friends and brethren; a rare example and worthy to be remembered."[91]

Of the *Mayflower's* original 102 passengers, 50 of them—nearly half of all who first began the voyage—died during their first winter at Plymouth. And while no one could have imagined such devastating losses at the start of their journey, the Pilgrims knew that God was with them—and, as Bradford wrote, their cause was worth the risk.

ABOVE: Two panels list the names of the Mayflower passengers, including the name of original member Robert Cushman, who arrived later on the Fortune in 1621. **BELOW:** A panoramic view from the top of Burial Hill in Plymouth, where many of the early Pilgrims are buried including Governor William Bradford, and William and Mary Brewster.

The original passengers of the Mayflower

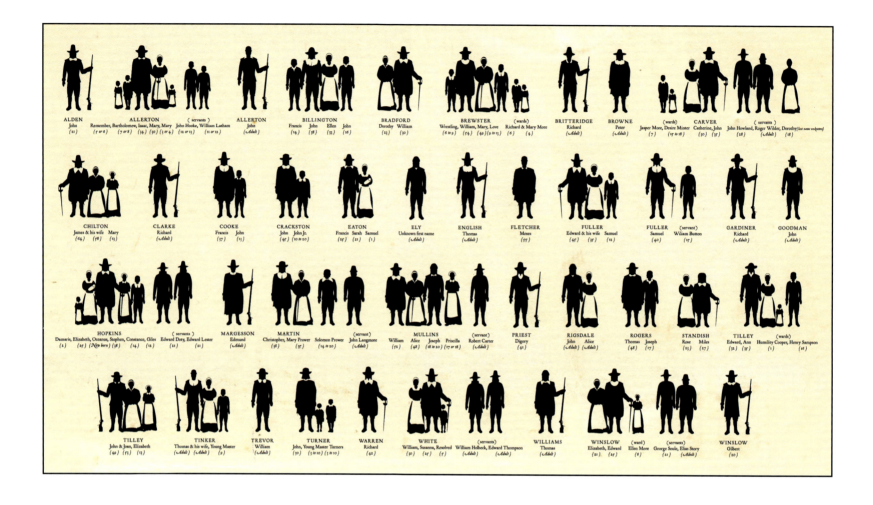

"It was replied that all great and honorable actions are accompanied with great difficulties, and must be both met and overcome with answerable courage. It was granted the dangers were great, but not desperate; the difficulties were many, but not invincible. For many of the things feared might never befall; others, by provident care and the use of good means, might in a great measure be prevented; and all of them, through the help of God, by fortitude and patience, might either be borne or overcome."

Those who survived to celebrate the first Thanksgiving of 1621

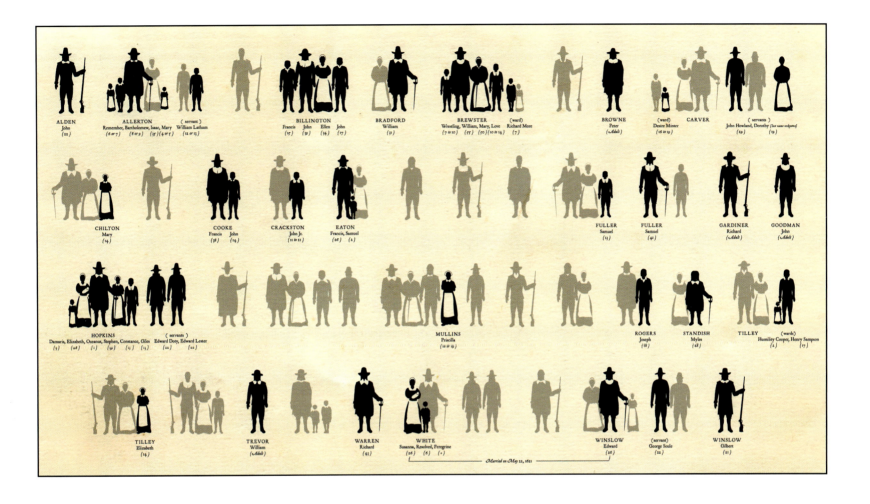

True it was that such attempts were not to be undertaken without good ground and reason, rashly or lightly; or, as many had done, for curiosity or hope of gain. But their condition was not ordinary; their ends were good and honorable; their calling, lawful and urgent; therefore they might expect the blessing of God on their proceedings. Yea, though they should lose their lives in this action, yet might they have the comfort in knowing that their endeavor was worthy." [92]

~ *William Bradford*

"The religion which has introduced civil liberty is the religion of Christ and His apostles, which enjoins humility, piety, and benevolence; which acknowledges in every person a brother, or a sister, and a citizen with equal rights. This is genuine Christianity, and to this we owe our free Constitutions of Government."

- Noah Webster (1758-1843), American lexicographer, English-language spelling reformer, textbook pioneer, considered the "Father of American Scholarship and Education"

LAW

ABOVE: Law was the last figure to be placed which completed the monument.

INSTALLED:
November 1888

ORDER:
Law was the last of the five allegorical figures to be set in place.

COST:
$10,000

SPONSOR:
Private donations led by Connecticut attorneys and the American Law Association, combined with an unused balance of $1,500 from a Federal grant that was issued for Liberty.

DESIGNER:
Working from original drawings by Hammatt Billings (1818-74), Morality was modeled by sculptor J.H. Mahoney (1855-1919).

HEIGHT:
Approximately 14 ft.

WEIGHT:
21 tons, cut from a single block.

LOWER MARBLE BAS-RELIEF PANEL:
Treaty with Massasoit was modeled by sculptor J.H. Mahoney (1855-1919), and sponsored by private donations from Connecticut lawyers and the balance of the Federal grant for Liberty.

As the first male figure to appear in the monument, Law appears serious and authoritative—an apt demeanor for the rules of conduct that are required to maintain a peaceful, orderly society. In one hand he holds the Rule of Law, and with the other, Law administers judgment by extending a hand in mercy.

When the Mayflower sailed off course into the waters of Cape Cod, the Pilgrims found themselves well outside the bounds of their legal jurisdiction. Their Virginia land patent held no power in this new territory, and the only recognized authority was vested in Captain Jones onboard the ship. When the Pilgrims considered abandoning their Virginia charter for a new life in Plymouth, certain *"Strangers"* onboard the ship—passengers not part of the Leiden congregation—resisted the idea. Some even threatened to go off on their own once they reached land and claimed no one had the power to stop them. They were right.

In his written history of Plymouth colony, Bradford recorded the fragile state of this early coalition onboard the ship. "This was occasioned partly by the discontented and mutinous speeches that some of the strangers amongst them had let fall: that when they got ashore they would use their liberty that none had power to command them, the patent procured being for Virginia, and not for New England, which belonged to another company, with which the Virginia company had nothing to do."[93] Everyone was essential if they hoped to survive in the wilderness, and with threats of a rising mutiny—the Pilgrims faced a crisis of attrition before they even left the ship. With no valid land charter and no recognized authority to guide them once they reached land, it begged the question—*who was in charge?*

To solve this problem, the Pilgrims relied on their experience as a church congregation. From their earliest meetings in Scrooby to their time spent in Leiden—the Pilgrims governed themselves independently as a church. Members freely "joined themselves together by covenant as a church," and swore a solemn oath to walk in all of God's ways.[94] The congregation chose its leaders, and even the decision to leave for America was decided by a majority vote. As the Pilgrim's pastor, John Robinson wrote, "We are knit together as a body in a most strict and sacred bond and covenant of the Lord, of the violation whereof we make great conscience, and by virtue whereof we hold ourselves straitly tied to all care of each other's good."[95]

ABOVE: *In his unrivaled series, "The Pageant of a Nation," American painter Jean Leon Gerome Ferris (1863–1930) portrays 78 pivotal scenes in American history. Here, Ferris depicts the 1620 signing of the Mayflower Compact in the cabin of the Mayflower.*

MAYFLOWER COMPACT

With this history in mind, the origins of the Mayflower Compact are much more apparent. Even though the Pilgrims—known as the *Saints*—comprised a minority of the ship's passengers, they were the only ones on the *Mayflower* with any experience in self-government based on their practices as a church.

For most of the ship's passengers, any ideas of government stemmed from their knowledge of the British monarchy. For these secular merchants, skilled workers, and adventurers—known as *Strangers* by the Pilgrims—the notion of self-government was utterly foreign. Still, the Pilgrims went to work. Together, they began drafting a new document to replace their obsolete land patent that would unite all the passengers onboard the ship. In this binding agreement, the signers freely swore an oath before God and each other and agreed to submit themselves to the duly elected laws and leadership of the new settlement— enacted for the good of all. Sound familiar?

On November 11, 1620, the Mayflower Compact was signed in the main cabin of the ship by forty-one men to represent every household in the new colony. And with this, the passengers of the *Mayflower*—both *Saints* and *Strangers* alike—joined themselves as a community of equals for self-government in the new world.

In doing so, the colonists "succeeded in establishing a self-governing community without benefit of a royal charter, royal proprietor, or corporate overlord, and… evinced an early political maturity which was not matched in any other American colony."[96] Written in the language of Biblical covenant, the Mayflower Compact reveals the influence of faith in establishing the new settlement that would later be known as Plymouth colony:

> *"In the name of God, Amen. Having undertaken, for the Glory of God, and advancements of the Christian faith, and the honor of our King and Country… a voyage to plant the first colony in the Northern parts of Virginia… do by these presents, solemnly and mutually, in the presence of God, and one another… covenant and combine ourselves together into a civil body politic."*[97]

> "The word *covenant* is not in common usage today as it was at the time of our founding. A covenant is a solemn agreement, or sacred promise, signed or not, between God and an individual, or individuals, a church, or a nation. Our Founders understood the power of covenants because they were Biblicists. They knew that God would inevitably act in accordance with His Word if the human covenanter would obey His Word. They also knew that this truth of blessing was applicable to a nation as well as to an individual. Deuteronomy 7:9 says: *"Know therefore that the Lord your God is God, the faithful God who keeps covenant and steadfast love with those who love Him and keep His commandments, to a thousand generations."*
>
> Source: *The American Covenant* by Marshall Foster

The Mayflower Compact

IN THE NAME OF GOD, AMEN. We, whose names are underwritten, the Loyal Subjects of our dread Sovereign Lord King James, by the Grace of God, of Great Britain, France, and Ireland, King, Defender of the Faith, &c. Having undertaken for the Glory of God, and Advancement of the Christian Faith, and the Honour of our King and Country, a Voyage to plant the first Colony in the northern Parts of Virginia; Do by these Presents, solemnly and mutually, in the Presence of God and one another, covenant and combine ourselves together into a civil Body Politick, for our better Ordering and Preservation, and Furtherance of the Ends aforesaid: And by Virtue hereof do enact, constitute, and frame, such just and equal Laws, Ordinances, Acts, Constitutions, and Officers, from time to time, as shall be thought most meet and convenient for the general Good of the Colony; unto which we promise all due Submission and Obedience. IN WITNESS whereof we have hereunto subscribed our names at Cape-Cod the eleventh of November, in the Reign of our Sovereign Lord King James, of England, France, and Ireland, the eighteenth, and of Scotland the fifty-fourth, Anno Domini; 1620.

TOP LEFT: *The oldest known copy of the Mayflower Compact is found in William Bradford's history of the colony, later published in the book, "Of Plimoth Plantation." This is the complete text of the original 1620 compact, as recorded by Bradford in his journal.*

> Plymouth Colony was the first experiment in consensual government in Western history between individuals with one another, and not with a monarch.
>
> Source: *The Mayflower: The Families, the Voyage and the Founding of America* by Rebecca Fraser

For perhaps the first time in human history, a group of individuals had freely consented to their own self-government. Such a rare act of democracy had little precedent. As author Jay Milbrandt writes: "The Mayflower Compact was an experiment—born out of necessity, but an experiment no less. They needed a local government, and they needed to maintain the whole of their enterprise. For this experiment, they had no template—a government formed contractually by the consent of the governed was revolutionary. For much of the world, and England in particular, monarchy and feudalism reigned as the practiced form of rule. The Separatists and the Strangers had never seen, nor experienced, an official democratic process. Yet Carver and Brewster had studied the classics of literature and philosophy. The opportunity to thoughtfully craft a new approach for the New World excited them."[98]

> Their deep faith in God—a God who they reverently believed held a special place in his heart for the Saints—profoundly affected all aspects of the administration of criminal justice in the ensuing years and left its imprint on the laws now directing the wheels of justice in the Commonwealth of Massachusetts.
>
> Source: *Crime and Punishment In Early Massachusetts, 1620-1692* by Edwin Powers

In 1802, a then-Senator John Quincy Adams was invited to speak at an anniversary celebration of the Pilgrim's landing in Plymouth. At this gathering, this future president famously heralded the Mayflower Compact, citing it as "perhaps the only instance, in human history, of that positive, original social compact, which speculative philosophers have imagined as the only legitimate source of government."[99] Revolutionary in its conception, this groundbreaking document would become an inspiration for many later constitutions—and pave the way for America's future constitutional republic.

TO RESTRAIN EVIL AND TO ADVANCE GOOD

The Pilgrims believed that lawful government was established by God to restrain evil and to advance good on the earth. As Christians, they were instructed to "be subject to the governing authorities, for there is no authority except that which God has established. The authorities that exist have been established by God." (Romans 13:1) By signing their names to the Mayflower Compact, the Pilgrims understood they were submitting to a civil order established by God for their own good.

At Plymouth Colony, the Pilgrims affirmed God's design for government by vowing to create "just and equal laws, ordinances, acts, constitutions, and offices" to serve the greater good of all.[100] The Pilgrims were heavily influenced by prominent Reformation leaders such as John Calvin and Martin Luther. Both Calvin and Luther articulated the idea that civil governments were established by God to restrain man's sinful nature and create a peaceful society where everyone was free to worship God.

ABOVE: *The official 1858 presidential portrait of John Quincy Adams by artist George Peter Alexander Healy. As the oldest son of John and Abigail Adams, John Quincy Adams grew up surrounded by his father's peers—men such as Benjamin Franklin and Thomas Jefferson. John Adams spoke of the close bond between his son and dear friend, writing that "he (John Quincy) seemed as much your (Thomas Jefferson's) son as mine." Traveling with his sons to Holland one year, Adams stayed in a house behind Pieterskerk, the Leiden church where many of the Pilgrims were buried. Visiting the Pieterskerk with his father left an impression on young John Quincy, and a deacon later attested that the elder Adams "could not refrain from tears" as he toured the cathedral. Growing up during the American Revolution, John Quincy Adams was keenly aware that the price of freedom was sacrifice—and he viewed the early Pilgrims with great reverence.*

The Pilgrim's pastor, John Robinson, also reminded them of God's Divine purpose for government. In early letters to his congregation, Pastor Robinson urged them to use wisdom when selecting leaders for their new settlement. "Lastly, whereas you are to become a body politic, administering among yourselves civil government, and are furnished with persons of no special eminence above the rest, from whom you will elect some to the office of government, let your wisdom and godliness appear, not only in choosing such persons as will entirely love and promote the common good, but also in yielding them all due honour and obedience in their lawful administrations; not beholding in them the ordinariness of their persons, but God's ordinance for your own good."[101]

RULE OF LAW

In 17th century England, any British citizen knew full well that "the law gave no protection to an innocent man. He might be thrown into jail at the pleasure of a high officer, tortured, and if brought to trial denied the assistance of counsel or the right to confront his witnesses. The judge held his job at the pleasure of the crown, while the jury well knew that they would be punished themselves if they gave a verdict contrary to what the queen desired."[102] To promote an equal society and prevent the abuse of power at Plymouth Colony, the Pilgrims instituted the *Rule of Law* to reflect their Biblical belief that "with the Lord our God there is no injustice or partiality or bribery." (2 Chronicles 19:7) As a principle, the Rule of Law was the idea that all citizens are accountable to the same laws—regardless of their position, power, or influence. Although the concept had been articulated much earlier in the Magna Carta of 1218, the principle had been erratically enforced across England. The Pilgrims suffered greatly under England's system of absolute power and politicized justice, and the *Rule of Law* would become a distinct feature of their new colony.

"As time would admit they met and consulted of law and order, both for civil and military government, as seemed suited to their conditions, adding to them from time to time as urgent need demanded. In these arduous and difficult beginnings, discontent and murmuring arose amongst some, and mutinous speech and bearing in others; but they were soon quelled and overcome by the wisdom, patience, and just and equal administration of things by the Governor and the better part, who held faithfully together in the main."

- William Bradford

> "Dozens of court records tell a similar tale. Those in positions of power and influence—up to and including the Governor himself—were all expected to live under the same laws."

Guided by the principles of the Mayflower Compact, the colonists proceeded to choose their leaders. John Carver was elected to be the colony's first Governor, along with several Assistants who would serve alongside him. Officers were appointed to oversee the colony's judicial and legislative affairs in a General Court. Early court records show that the Pilgrims endeavored to apply the law equally in their new settlement. "That no one was above the law can be seen in the 1636 conviction of Stephen Hopkins, who was at the time an Assistant and magistrate himself, but still was fined £5 for battery against John Tisdale, the court observing that Hopkins should have especially been one to observe the king's peace."[103] In this instance, not only was Hopkins held to account despite his powerful office—but it appears the judge expected a higher standard of conduct from him precisely *because* of it.

Dozens of court records tell a similar tale. Those in positions of power and influence—up to and including the Governor himself—were all expected to live under the same laws. "In some cases in Plymouth it can be deduced that (Governor) Bradford and other high officials were not above the law by what did not happen rather than what did. In October 1636 Bradford went to court to charge four men with trespass; that he won his case is not so important as the fact that he had to go to the court in the first place, for he was not powerful enough on his own to get his way."[104] Sixteen years after their settlement was founded, William Bradford had become one of Plymouth Colony's most respected and influential leaders. That the Governor himself appealed to the rule of law is compelling—and reveals much about his character and the Pilgrim code of ethics.

ABOVE: *In 1920, a half-dollar coin was struck to mark the Tercentenary, the 300-year anniversary of the Pilgrim's arrival in Plymouth. Designed by sculptor Cyrus Edwin Dallin, the front depicted Governor Bradford with a Bible under his arm, and featured the Mayflower on the reverse. The value of these commemorative coins has steadily increased, with some coins selling for hundreds of dollars in 1980. In 2014, an exceptional coin from this 1920 commemorative issuance sold at auction for $7,344.*

LEFT: *A vintage postcard depicts Governor Bradford's home in 1621.*

> "The Pilgrim policy was to purchase land from the natives. They did not buy the site for Plymouth Plantation from the Patuxets because only one was living after the epidemic that swept thousands away. The surviving Patuxet, Squanto, might have reaped some compensation... but he died in 1622. Most of the land in Plymouth Colony was bought from the tribes. Massasoit offered them land. The Pilgrims insisted on paying the Indian owners. In an effort to protect the natives from exploitation, the General Court ordered in 1643 that no one could purchase land without court approval. At the beginning there was a sincere effort to play fairly and to check exploitation. The first registry of deeds in the New World was set up to handle land transactions. Deeds were filed with an official of the colony. Full recognition of the Indians' title was required."
>
> Source: *The Faith Of The Pilgrims* by Robert M. Bartlett

1636 PILGRIM CODE OF LAW

As Plymouth Colony grew and its territory expanded, all its existing laws were compiled into a single volume for greater clarity. In 1636, the General Court of Plymouth published the Pilgrim Code of Law, an extraordinary compilation that would become the first instance of legal code produced in America. Effectively defining the laws of Plymouth Colony, the 1636 Pilgrim Code of Law outlined the role of government, detailed the requirements for every civic office, and secured a bill of rights for its citizens—an feat that eclipsed Massachusetts Bay and earlier Virginia colonies.

As author and legal scholar George Haskins writes, this 1636 Code of Law was remarkable in several ways. "In the first place, the code sets forth the general scheme or frame of government of the colony: the source of legislative power, the duties and authority of the several officers of the colony, qualifications for the franchise, provision for the holding of courts, and the source of authority to declare war. Second, it contains a rudimentary bill of rights, certainly the first in America… nothing that was attempted earlier in Virginia was of the same scope; there the so-called constitution was chiefly composed of orders and instructions directed at, but not established by, the colonists, and certainly it included nothing that might be termed a general bill of rights."[105]

The Pilgrim Code of Law guaranteed the right of each citizen to a system of impartial justice—which included due process and a trial by jury. "Much more than a code of law, this document lays out the fundamental values and political institutions of the community and is a candidate for the honor of being the first true written constitution in the modern world."[106] Encapsulating the first sixteen years of legal history in the new settlement, the Pilgrim Code of Law offers a fascinating glimpse into early colonial life.

TOP: *At the Plimoth-Patuxet Museum in Plymouth, Massachusetts, a living re-enactment of the early settlement allows visitors to step back into the 17th century and imagine life as a Pilgrim at Plymouth Colony.* **BOTTOM LEFT:** *An illustration depicts the Old Fort and First Meeting House of Plymouth Colony in 1621.* **BOTTOM CENTER:** *A vintage postcard reveals a montage of early Pilgrim landmarks, including Clark's Island, Burial Hill, and the first homes built in 1622.* **BOTTOM RIGHT:** *In "Sailing of the Mayflower," the Pilgrims gather in somber reflection as the Mayflower departs Plymouth harbor to begin its journey home to England. Despite the incredible offer of free passage from Captain Jones, every Pilgrim chose to remain at their new home in America.*

"The earliest Plymouth laws reflect concern about basic problems common to all communities: landholding, the inheritance of property, marriage, crime, court proceedings, and the like. As time went on and the colony grew, the laws reflected not only the maturing social organization, but local problems and conditions, such as those involved in legislation about bridges and ferries, highways, fairs, weights and measures, price and wage control, licensing of innkeepers, the quality of exports, and provision for the poor."[107] Many early Pilgrim laws were guided by Biblical principles of morality and justice. "For the first few years they administered justice with considerable informality but with a relatively rare degree of humanity."[108] According to early court records, magistrates appointed to enforce the colony's laws appeared more interested in deterrence than exacting harsh punishment. "The practice of justice was more humane in Plymouth than in many areas of the world at that period. Plymouth never employed torture, never burned a criminal alive, never punished a witch, never applied the cruel practices that were common in other countries. A very small number found guilty of murder were hanged."[109]

What is Plymouth's Lot One?

ABOVE: *A modern view of Leyden Street, the first street established by the Pilgrims at Plymouth Colony.* **RIGHT**: *An early glimpse of this historic road circa 1900.* **BELOW**: *Early maps of Plymouth Colony detail its original layout, including First Street (renamed Leyden Street), the Common House, and the first homes built by the Pilgrims.*

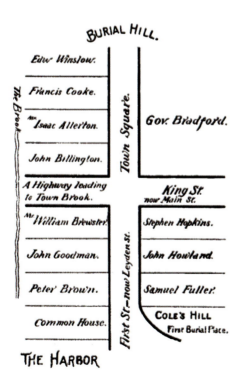

HISTORIC LEYDEN STREET

As the oldest street in Plymouth—and arguably, of the original thirteen colonies— Leyden Street was the first street established by the Pilgrims when they began constructing homes on land. Originally known as First Street, early town documents also refer to it as Great Street and Broad Street. In 1823, it was officially renamed Leyden Street in tribute to the Pilgrim's time in Holland. Although none of the early structures survive, the current layout of 18th and 19th-century homes approximates the original design of the early settlement. *(See map on left)* As the Pilgrims divided up the land to build homes, the first lot was designated for use as a Common House—and Plymouth town records refer to this parcel as Lot #1.

Today, this site is located at 33 Leyden Street and listed on the National Register of Historic Places. On February 27, 1621, it was here that Myles Standish was elected Captain of the colony by a majority vote. On April 21, 1621, it was also on or near this site that Governor Carver signed the famous peace treaty with Chief Massasoit. The historical legacy of Lot #1 is stewarded by the Leyden Preservation Group, a non-profit organization that works to preserve historical sites which foster a greater understanding of the unique American identity that began at Plymouth Colony in 1620. To learn more, visit 400th.org.

TRADITION MEETS INNOVATION

Although the Pilgrims kept many familiar traditions of English common law, they also demonstrated the influence of their time in Holland by adopting the Dutch practice of civil marriage. But even so, "their law was their own law, a mixture of Biblical and common-law origins, frequently more liberal and progressive than the law of England at that time."[110] By combining their own experiences with Biblical wisdom and innovation, the Pilgrims fashioned a unique code of law that has made "lasting contributions to the present-day law of Massachusetts and, ultimately, to the modern law of the United States."[111]

Women enjoyed considerable legal rights at Plymouth Colony compared to their English counterparts. In 17th century England, women were rarely recognized outside of marriage. They seldom owned property or engaged in legal contracts apart from a husband. If a married man died intestate—without leaving a valid will behind—his widow was only entitled to one-third of her late husband's land. By contrast, a widow at Plymouth under these same circumstances was entitled to one-third of her late husband's land, goods and personal property—a sizable increase. Women could also petition the General Court over a perceived "unfair" will, and court records show that judges often intervened to increase a widow's inheritance for a good cause. Court records also reveal that women frequently signed legal contracts on their own—independent of a husband. Women played a vital role in Plymouth Colony, and its legal rulings reflect that.

> "The practice of justice was more humane in Plymouth than in many areas of the world at that period. Plymouth never employed torture, never burned a criminal alive, never punished a witch, never applied the cruel practices that were common in other countries. A very small number found guilty of murder were hanged."
>
> Source: *The Faith Of The Pilgrims* by Robert Merrill Bartlett

LEFT: In 1924, the statue entitled "Pilgrim Maiden" was erected by the National Society of New England Women to honor the pioneering women of Plymouth Colony.

BELOW: Displayed in Brewster Gardens near the Plymouth waterfront, its dedication panel reads: "To those intrepid English women whose courage, fortitude and devotion brought a new nation into being, this statue of the Pilgrim Maiden is dedicated."

ABOVE: *In 17th century England, the common practice of primogeniture entitled each firstborn male to inherit his family's entire estate. Pictured above is Highclere Castle in Hampshire, a 5,000-acre estate which gained acclaim as the site of "Downton Abbey," the popular British drama set in the early 20th century. Estates such as these would inevitably be inherited by the oldest male in the family.*

The Pilgrims were also advanced in their laws concerning children. In England, the legal practice of *primogeniture* was widely applied—a tradition that entitled the firstborn male in each family to inherit his family's entire estate. The Pilgrims rejected this practice at Plymouth Colony. Instead, they enacted the law of *partible descent*—a practice that divided a family's estate equally among all children while granting a double portion to the oldest. In this way, the Pilgrims sought to apply greater fairness under the law while still honoring the Biblical tradition of granting firstborns a double portion.

The Pilgrim's record of enacting laws to protect the weak and marginalized ran well ahead of their contemporaries, including areas such as "civil marriage, equality of descent among children, provision for widows, and recording of deeds. All these were marked advances on English law."[112]

MERCY

On the right side of *Law's* seated pedestal, *Mercy* appears with both hands lifted in a posture of humility— as if he is pleading for leniency. Even as the Pilgrims worked diligently to enact "just and equal laws… for the general good of the colony," they also believed it was their duty to "act justly and to love mercy and to walk humbly with your God." (Micah 6:8) Although capital punishment was enforced at Plymouth Colony, it was administered infrequently and reserved for the most heinous of crimes—such as willful murder.

> "Learn to do good; seek justice, correct oppression; bring justice to the fatherless, plead the widow's cause."
>
> - Isaiah 1:17

> But when he grew weak they had compassion on him and helped him. Then he confessed he did not deserve it at their hands, for he had abused them in word and deed. "Oh," said he, *"I see now you show your love like Christians indeed to one another; but we let one another lie and die like dogs."*

For the Pilgrims, mercy was not only a crucial balance in the courtroom but a Biblical mandate for daily life. When the *Mayflower* dropped anchor in Plymouth harbor, cold weather had already set in as the Pilgrims raced to build shelters on land. Soon, many became ill due to a "powerful combination of scurvy, pneumonia, and tuberculosis…brought on by months of bad diet, cramped and unsanitary quarters, exposure and overexertion in all kinds of weather."[113]

Sick passengers were cruelly kicked off the ship—and forced to risk drinking contaminated water on land while the crew hoarded the ship's supply of beer for themselves. When one sick passenger begged for even a tiny cup of beer to safely quench his thirst, one sailor callously replied, *"If you were my own father I wouldn't give you any!"*

But disease soon spread among the sailors, so that "almost half of the crew died before they went away, and many of their officers and strongest men, amongst them the boatswain, gunner, three quartermasters, the cook and others."[114] A crew once consisting of healthy, robust sailors—was now comprised of weak men languishing in their sickbeds—cursing, complaining, and ruing the day they ever set foot on the ship.

TOP: *The Mayflower II, a modern replica of the original 17th-century ship, is moored on Plymouth's historic waterfront. Here, visitors can tour the vessel and imagine the impossibly small space where 102 passengers lived for over ten weeks at sea during the Mayflower's 1620 voyage to America.* **RIGHT:** *A scale model of a 17th-century English merchant ship similar to the Mayflower of 1620.*

Why was beer such a valuable commodity on the Mayflower?

In the 17th century, whether you were embarking on a long sea journey or exploring unknown territories on land—clean drinking water was often challenging to find. The passengers on the Mayflower drank a type of low-alcohol beer called ale, which was considered a safe, even nutritious alternative when freshwater was unavailable. Weakly brewed from barley, ale produced almost a "liquid bread"— a calorie-rich beverage that supplied hydration and energy. These benefits, coupled with the constant danger of drinking water contaminated with disease-causing bacteria, explain why beer was such a treasured item onboard the ship. As the Mayflower's supply of food and safe drinking water dwindled, many passengers rightly viewed beer as their last defense against dehydration, starvation, and disease.

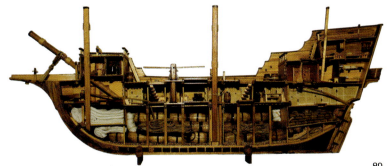

Good friends who once sang and drank together in jolly camaraderie now viewed their infected shipmates with scorn, muttering—*"If they die, let them die!"* Seeing his crew in shambles, Captain Jones relented. He sent word to the Pilgrims on land and allowed them to return to the *Mayflower* for shelter and supplies. After reboarding the ship, the Pilgrims began caring for the ailing sailors and nursed many back to health. They demonstrated such mercy and compassion to the same men who had treated them so cruelly just days earlier—that it elicited a deathbed conversion from one sailor in his final hours of life. "But the passengers who were still aboard showed them what pity they could, which made some of their hearts relent, such as the boatswain, who was an overbearing young man, and before would often curse and scoff at the passengers. But when he grew weak they had compassion on him and helped him. Then he confessed he did not deserve it at their hands, for he had abused them in word and deed. "Oh," said he, "I see now you show your love like Christians indeed to one another; but we let one another lie and die like dogs."[115]

JUSTICE

To the left of *Law's* pedestal, the image of *Justice* is shown in her familiar form—with scales in one hand and a sword in the other. Traditionally, scales represent the weighing of evidence or truth, and a sword is symbolic of authority or final judgment. At Plymouth colony, the Pilgrims endeavored to provide equal justice under the law, believing they were called to "Hate evil, love good; (and) maintain justice in the courts." (Amos 5:15) In all legal deliberations, the Pilgrims enforced due process and applied a Biblical standard of using at least two or three witnesses to ascertain what was true.

In 1638, this practice was highlighted when several men were arrested for the robbery and murder of a native Indian. Arthur Peach, the group's ringleader, was a former soldier whom William Bradford described as "out of means and loth to work, and taking to idle ways and company."[116] After seducing a maidservant and running up several personal debts, Peach skipped town with friends and traveled from Massachusetts Bay into Narragansetts' country.

"He appointed judges in the land, in each of the fortified cities of Judah. He told them, "Consider carefully what you do, because you are not judging for mere mortals but for the Lord, who is with you whenever you give a verdict. Now let the fear of the Lord be on you. Judge carefully, for with the Lord our God there is no injustice or partiality or bribery."

-2 Chronicles 19:5-7

Along their journey, they stopped to rest by the side of the footpath. It was here, casually smoking tobacco around a fire, that Peach and his friends looked up to see an Indian they recognized from the day before. "At length there came a Narragansett Indian by, who had been trading at the Bay, and had some cloth and beads with him. They had met him the day before, and now he was returning. Peach called him to come and drink tobacco with them, and he came and sat down. He had told the others he would kill the Indian and take his goods. The others were afraid; but Peach said, 'Hang the rogue, he has killed many of us.' So they let him do as he would, and when he saw his opportunity, he took his rapier and ran the man through the body once or twice, and took from him five fathoms of wampum and three coats of cloth; and then they went their way, leaving him for dead."[117]

ABOVE: *A rare image of the monument at night, under the beautiful silhouette of a starry evening sky.*

This vicious attack would have gone unpunished, except that incredibly—"the Indian managed to scramble up when they had gone, and made shift to get home."[118] Staggering to reach members of his tribe, the victim lived long enough to identify his assailants—setting others off in quick pursuit. When the Indians eventually captured Peach and his accomplices, they demanded justice, and the case was sent to Plymouth for a trial. The jury delivered a guilty verdict, and the men were hanged. According to William Bradford, justice was served over the objections of certain "rude and ignorant" colonists.

"Nevertheless, some of the more ignorant colonists objected that an Englishman should be put to death for an Indian. So at last the murderers were brought home… and after being tried and the evidence produced, they all in the end freely confessed to all the Indian had accused them of, and that they had done it in the manner described. So they were condemned by the jury, and executed. Some of the Narragansett Indians and the murdered man's friends were present when it was done, which gave them and all the country satisfaction. But it was a matter of much sadness to them here, as it was the second execution since they came—both being for willful murder."[119]

Bradford's narrative of the event is compelling. By describing some colonists as "ignorant," he affirms the moral superiority of the Rule of Law— and securing equal justice. Similarly, when he writes that "all the country" took satisfaction in the guilty verdict and corresponding punishment, Bradford demonstrates that "when justice is done, it is a joy to the righteous but terror to evildoers." (Proverbs 21:15) His mention of sadness over the incident is also quite telling. Although the Pilgrims knew "all have sinned and fall short of the glory of God," it obviously grieved them to see others reject God's gift of grace "through the redemption that is in Christ Jesus." (Romans 3:23-24) But despite their sorrow over such a vicious act of calculated murder—the Pilgrims proved they were committed to equal justice under the law.

> What is particularly impressive, however, is the evidence which appears early and persistently in the Plymouth enactments and court records, that the colonists were governed by and lived under a rule of law. Few ideas have had so profound or so pervasive an influence in Anglo-American jurisprudence as has the idea that no man is above the law. It has crystallized in the doctrine of the "rule" or "supremacy" of law, which has long been regarded as one of the central and most characteristic features of the Western legal tradition.
>
> Source; *The Legal Heritage Of Plymouth Colony* by George L. Haskins

MARBLE BAS-RELIEF PANEL: TREATY WITH MASSASOIT

Relying on Squanto as their translator, the Pilgrims were able to arrange an important meeting with Chief Massasoit, the grand sachem of the Wampanoag Indian tribe. When Chief Massasoit arrived at Plymouth colony, Governor Carver greeted him with great ceremony and respect—and showered him with gifts and entertainment.

This diplomatic encounter resulted in the *Pilgrim-Wampanoag Peace Treaty*, in which both parties agreed to the following terms:

1. That neither he nor any of his, should injure or harm any of their people.
2. That if any of his did any harm to any of theirs, he should send the offender, that they might punish him.
3. That if anything were taken away from any of theirs, he should cause it to be restored; and they should do the like to his.
4. If any made unjust war against him, they would aid him; and if any made war against them, he should aid them.
5. He should send to his neighboring confederates to certify them of this, that they might not wrong them, but might be likewise comprised in the conditions of peace.
6. That when their men came to them, they should leave their bows and arrows behind them.

RIGHT: *A life-size figure honoring Massasoit stands majestically on Cole's Hill overlooking the Plymouth harbor. This statue was produced in 1921 by American sculptor Cyrus Edwin Dallin for the Tercentenary, the 300th anniversary of the Pilgrim's arrival in Plymouth. Several replicas are on display across the nation, including one at Utah's State Capital.*

The alliance was strategic for both sides. The powerful Narragansett Indian tribe threatened the Wampanoags, and this new treaty offered Chief Massasoit crucial military support from the Pilgrims. The treaty ensured mutual peace for the colonists, and Squanto chose to remain in his old village— providing invaluable help to the Pilgrims. "Squanto stayed with them, and was their interpreter, and became a special instrument sent of God for their good, beyond their expectation. He showed them how to plant their corn, where to take fish and other commodities, and guided them to unknown places, and never left them till he died."[120] Shortly after the peace treaty was signed, Governor Carver unexpectedly died, and William Bradford was elected to replace him. In a remarkable tribute to the leadership of both Governor Bradford and Chief Massasoit, the agreement prevailed despite Carver's death. Incredibly, the peace treaty was honored and remained intact for over 50 years.

In his book, *The Pilgrim Chronicles,* author Rod Gragg writes: "Massasoit's decision to make peace with the Pilgrims would prove critical to the survival of Plymouth Colony. At the time of the treaty, the Pilgrims could muster barely twenty men to serve in the colony's militia. Despite their firearms and artillery, they were massively outnumbered by the Indians. Why did Massasoit not order a massacre of the Pilgrims and wipe out the weak, struggling colony in its infancy? Why was Plymouth spared the repeated attacks and bloodshed that marked the early history of Virginia's Jamestown Colony? Was it the Pilgrims' generally respectful attitude toward the Native Americans, or the diplomacy they afforded Massasoit? Or did Chief Massasoit simply decide to exercise restraint? Again, to William Bradford, it was all an act of divine grace, in which 'the powerful hand of the Lord did protect them.' "[121]

LEFT/BELOW: *A life-size statue of Chief Massasoit is located on top of Cole's Hill in Plymouth, and features panoramic views of Plymouth Rock and the waterfront.*

Massasoit's plaque features the following dedication:

MASSASOIT GREAT SACHEM OF THE WAMPANOAGS PROTECTOR AND PRESERVER OF THE PILGRIMS 1621

"The Pilgrims: a simple people, inspired by an ardent faith in God, a dauntless courage in danger, a boundless resourcefulness in the face of difficulties, and impregnable fortitude in adversity; thus they have in some measure become the spiritual ancestors of all Americans."

- Samuel Eliot Morison, author, historian, Harvard professor and editor of William Bradford's *Of Plimoth Plantation*

In his recorded history of the new settlement, William Bradford detailed the Pilgrim's reasoning and motivations for establishing a new colony in America.

"First I will unfold the causes that led to the foundation of the New Plymouth Settlement, and the motives of those concerned in it. In order that I may give an accurate account of the project, I must begin at the very root and rise of it; and this I shall endeavour to do in a plain style and with singular regard to the truth,—at least as near as my slender judgment can attain to it."

"It was replied that all great and honorable actions are accompanied with great difficulties, and must be both met and overcome with answerable courage. It was granted the dangers were great, but not desperate; the difficulties were many, but not invincible. For many of the things feared might never befall; others, by provident care and the use of good means, might in a great measure be prevented; and all of them, through the help of God, by fortitude and patience, might either be borne or overcome. True it was that such attempts were not to be undertaken without good ground and reason, rashly or lightly; or, as many had done, for curiosity or hope of gain. But their condition was not ordinary; their ends were good and honorable; their calling, lawful and urgent; therefore they might expect the blessing of God on their proceedings. Yea, though they should lose their lives in this action, yet might they have the comfort in knowing that their endeavor was worthy."

"Last and not least, they cherished a great hope and inward zeal of laying good foundations, or at least of making some way towards it, for the propagation and advance of the gospel of the kingdom of Christ in the remote parts of the world, even though they should be but stepping stones to others in the performance of so great a work."

"Thus out of small beginnings greater things have been produced by his hand that made all things of nothing and gives being to all things that are; and as one small candle may light a thousand, so the light here kindled hath shone unto many, yea in some sort to our whole nation; let the glorious name of Jehovah have all the praise."

- Governor William Bradford

Source: *Bradford's History of the Plymouth Settlement, 1608-1650*

"Educate and inform the whole mass of the people... they are the only sure reliance for the preservation of our liberty."

- Thomas Jefferson (1743-1826), American Founding Father, principal author of the *Declaration of Independence* (1776), and the third President of the United States (1801–1809)

EDUCATION

INSTALLED:
October 7, 1881

ORDER:
Education was the third of the five allegorical figures to be placed.

COST:
$10,000

SPONSOR:
Roland Mather, Esq., of Hartford, Connecticut

DESIGNER:
Working from original drawings by Hammatt Billings (1818-74), *Education* was modeled by Alexander Doyle (1857-1922).

HEIGHT:
Approximately 15 ft.

WEIGHT:
Approximately 25 tons, cut from a single block.

LOWER MARBLE BAS-RELIEF PANEL:
Signing of the Compact was modeled by John M. Moffitt (1837-87), and sponsored by Roland Mather, Esq.

Stately and virtuous, the statue of *Education* is crowned with a victor's wreath to signify the honor of learning. She holds a book, presumably a Bible, and points to its open pages to emphasize the importance of gaining knowledge and cultivating intellect.

Most early Pilgrims came from humble backgrounds as merchants and laborers, and only a select few had received a university education. But as a church body, the congregation was intellectually curious and eager for knowledge. Many of the Pilgrim's spiritual leaders were university trained and imparted the traditions of higher learning to the congregation. The Pilgrims spent hours together in church discussing sermons and some of the most profound theological debates of their day. Whether it was achieved through formal education or the personal pursuit of knowledge, the Pilgrims believed that "the beginning of wisdom is this: Get wisdom. Though it cost all you have, get understanding." (Proverbs 4:7)

ABOVE: *Education was the third of the five figures to be set in place.*

PASTOR JOHN ROBINSON

Many early church reform leaders in the Separatist movement came from the halls of learning at Cambridge University. John Robinson, who would play an influential role in the Pilgrim story as their beloved pastor, was one of these leaders. Robinson came from a modest background and worked odd jobs to support himself as he studied ministry at the University's Corpus Christi College. "Bright and disciplined, he excelled at Cambridge, and—under the influence of some of the leading Puritan thinkers of the day—he embraced Puritan theology and became committed to reform the Church of England."[122]

After he earned his undergraduate and graduate degrees from Cambridge, Robinson "spent seven years on the Cambridge faculty, rising to the post of dean, then left the university to marry Bridget White, a farmer's daughter from his hometown."[123] Newly married and eager to start a family, Robinson accepted a position as Assistant Pastor for St. Andrew's Church in Norwich, then one of England's largest cities and a growing hub of Puritan support. "Studious, empathetic, and gentle in nature, Robinson had a pastor's heart and a preacher's gift for exposing the Word from the pulpit."[124] Tending to the needs of a busy congregation and his growing young family, Robinson found great contentment in this season of ministry.

By 1604, the clamor from Puritans wanting to "purify" the Anglican church of its unbiblical practices drew the ire of church officials. To clamp down on these Puritan reformers, the Archbishop ordered all clergy to swear allegiance to the new Book of Canons—a compilation of all church laws. As intended, this caused tremendous conflict for those who believed that many of the church's rules opposed Scripture. As one such clergyman, Robinson was forced to decide: "Could he continue in good conscience to serve the Church of England if its leadership indeed held what he believed to be unbiblical positions on key issues?"[125] The answer was no. For Robinson and others, their refusal to comply came from a place of deep faith—after great contemplation under enormous pressure. Asked to pledge allegiance to unbiblical church doctrine, they chose to obey conscience and Scripture over man's rules. "Along with hundreds of other Anglican pastors with Puritan leanings, Robinson was suspended from the ministry, and lost his position at St. Andrews Church."[126]

ABOVE: The historic pews and arches of an Anglican Church in 18th-century England. **RIGHT:** A morning mist lingers over a local church and farm buildings in the English countryside.

After being expelled from the Church of England, Robinson returned to the English countryside, "where the Separatist movement was growing in illegal congregations among the region's farmers, laborers, merchants, and landowners."[127] Through an acquaintance with William Brewster, Robinson was soon invited to join a small gathering of Separatists secretly meeting at Brewster's home in Scrooby, a tiny village outside of Nottinghamshire. It was here, at Scrooby Manor, that the earliest Pilgrims first gathered for worship under the leadership of Richard Clifton, a local pastor who had been stripped of his pastorate for preaching on reforms. Robinson joined this gathering at Scrooby Manor, where reform-minded individuals met secretly to pray, worship, and study the Bible together. In time, Clifton would invite Robinson to help him co-pastor the growing congregation.

Although most of the Pilgrims came from humble, working-class backgrounds, "the colonists, and especially their ministers, were thoroughly familiar with a wide range of theological writings, from the learned sermons of the most renowned ministers to the more systematic treatises of Calvin, Luther, and Knox."[128] Under the guidance of their university-trained leaders, the Pilgrims

> "Pinning their faith on the scriptures and on reason, the Pilgrims dared to grapple with the profundities of faith and controversial concepts like the sovereignty of God, predestination, salvation, eschatology, biblical exegesis, the nature of the church, and the limits of civil authority."
>
> Source: *The Faith of the Pilgrims* by Robert M. Bartlett

ABOVE: *The modern court of Corpus Christi College, one of thirty-one colleges that comprise the University of Cambridge, where John Robinson obtained his Bachelor of Arts degree in 1596.*

relished the opportunity to hear and discuss weighty sermons, and the church enjoyed spirited debates. "Pinning their faith on the scriptures and on reason, the Pilgrims dared to grapple with the profundities of faith and controversial concepts like the sovereignty of God, predestination, salvation, eschatology, biblical exegesis, the nature of the church, and the limits of civil authority."[129]

PILGRIM LEADERSHIP

As the spiritual leaders of the Pilgrims, Pastor John Robinson and Elder William Brewster each "brought the tradition of learning from Cambridge and influenced the people of Plymouth, who looked up to them as their intellectual and spiritual guides."[130] Likewise, although William Bradford never attended university, he was a curious, self-taught thinker and scholar. Indeed, Bradford was just fourteen when he first joined the Scrooby congregation, and the influence of Robinson and Brewster as mentors and father figures would have a profound impact on his life.

As a new convert to the faith, young William spent countless hours studying the Bible, Latin, and Greek with both men. Later, at Plymouth Colony, an older Bradford—now well into his forties and fully established in the office of Governor—kept a vast library for personal study and teaching. Bradford's impressive collection of books rivaled the 400 titles bequeathed by clergyman John Harvard to New College in Cambridge, Massachusetts, in 1636— a gift that caused the school to rename itself Harvard University in 1639 after their first great benefactor. Along with his treasured books, Bradford devoted his final years to learning Hebrew, the original language of the Old Testament. He wrote about this spiritual quest in his journal, saying that he longed:

"... to see with mine own eyes, something of that most ancient language... in which the law and oracles of God were write; and in which God and angels, spake to the holy patriarchs, of old time; and what names were given to things, from the creation." [131]

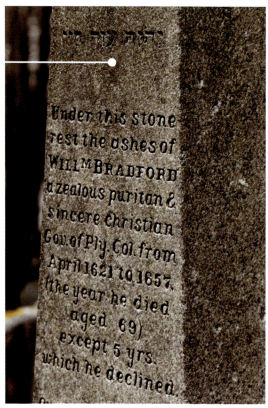

Hebrew translation in English: *"Jehovah is the help of my life"*

ABOVE: William Bradford is buried at Burial Hill Cemetery in Plymouth, a site which is featured on the National Register of Historic Places. Perched on a hill overlooking Plymouth harbor, Bradford's grave marker is comprised of a stone obelisk which pays tribute to his faith and love for the Hebrew language.

> Plymouth Colony residents were required to prepare a last will and testament. After death, an inventory of possessions was prepared and registered. These inventories offer insight into home life: the furniture, clothing, bedding, linen, pewter, pottery, utensils, equipment, tools, animals, and books. The plantation had a fair supply of the last item. *William Brewster* owned 393 books, 62 in Latin and the balance in English. An analysis of his library classified 98 books as expository, 63 as doctrinal, 69 as practical religion, 24 as historical, 38 as ecclesiastical, 6 as philosophical, 14 as poetical, and 54 as miscellaneous. Four books were by John Robinson. Eleven had been printed in Leyden by the Pilgrim Press. *William Bradford* also had at least four hundred volumes including works by Robins, Calvin, Luther, Peter Martyr, Cartwright, Cotton, and Ainsworth, and several works in Dutch. *Dr. Samuel Fuller* owned three Bibles, a psalm book, a concordance, a catechism, titles by Robinson and Ainsworth, dictionaries, works on the Bible, and sermons, along with his "Physicke Bookes" and "a Surgions chest with the things belonging to it." *Captain Myles Standish* had a surprising collection, in addition to titles of military science and history. He had three old Bibles, a New Testament, a psalm book, works of Calvin, Preston, Dod, Davenport, and Cotton, along with Homer's *Iliad*.
>
> Source: *The Faith Of The Pilgrims* by Robert M. Bartlett

Despite certain modern perceptions of colonial living, books were abundant at Plymouth Colony. "The number of volumes possessed by settlers in the colony was remarkable, considering the size of the community, the high price of books, and the scarcity of personally owned books in this era. Although admittedly some of these were heavy theology and beyond the grasp of the average colonist…the general distribution of the Bible and the Ainsworth psalter proves that the majority did read and had a vital interest in their religion."[132]

> For the Pilgrims, the Bible was the foundation for all education. Literacy was not only important so their children could read and understand Scripture for themselves—but also to protect their civil freedoms when government rulers proposed evil, unbiblical laws that could lead to tyranny.

Historical documents reveal that many Pilgrims had a strong command of Elizabethan English, including prominent leaders like Carver, Bradford, Brewster, Cushman, Allerton, and Winslow. Bradford and Winslow both were exceptionally gifted and prolific writers. Their literary talents would be invaluable in documenting the early history of Plymouth Colony. Bradford's journals—his "scribbled writings," as he referred to them—would eventually produce the time-honored American classic, *Of Plymouth Plantation*.

THE EDUCATION OF CHILDREN
There were no formal schools in the early years of Plymouth Colony, and children were educated primarily at home or with members of another family. The family unit acted as a school, as each child's education began "at the mother's knee, and often ended in the cornfield or barn by the father's side."[133] Following the wisdom of Scripture, the Pilgrims believed "the fear of the Lord is the beginning of knowledge." (Proverbs 1:7) They accepted their God-given role as parents to instill moral virtues in their children and impart practical skills that would enable them to be self-sufficient as they grew older.

In the early 17th century, one of the most widely read books on parenting was called *A Godly Forme of Household Government.* This popular guide captured the goal of Pilgrim parents to "instruct their children in the principles of religion, good manners, and civil behavior; to inculcate in them reverence for their elders and superiors; to bring them up in some lawful and gainful calling; to teach them to read and write for both worldly and spiritual ends."[134]

For the Pilgrims, the greatest aim of literacy was to enable their children to read so they could understand and interpret Scripture for themselves. Gathered around the family Bible, parents would help a child sound out letters and syllables phonetically—reciting passages of Scripture out loud until the connection between the oral and written word was eventually understood.

ABOVE: *In the 1897 colonial book, "History of the Horn-book," a young girl learns her alphabet using this early educational tool.*

Even young children were included in family devotions and grew up hearing the rich stories and moral lessons of Scripture. Together as a family, the Bible was "read and recited, quoted and consulted…committed to memory and constantly searched for meaning" each day in the home.[135] The process of instilling literacy, morals, and manners into children was incorporated into the daily routines of life. Armed with love and discipline, "colonial mothers often achieved more than our modern-day elementary schools with their federally-funded programs and education specialists. These colonial mothers used simple, time-tested methods of instruction mixed with plain, old-fashioned hard work."[136]

ABOVE: *A 1950's souvenir from Plymouth, Massachusetts, recreates the Horn Book, an educational primer used from the 16th to 19th century. Although they varied in style and substance, most Horn Books featured the alphabet and the Lord's Prayer and were often attached to a child's clothing with a cord to prevent them from losing it.*

"Every member of the State ought diligently to read and to study the constitution of his country, and teach the rising generation to be free. By knowing their rights, they will sooner perceive when they are violated, and be the better prepared to defend and assert them."

- John Jay (1745-1829), Founding Father, abolitionist, American statesman, First Chief Justice of the Supreme Court of the United States

What were common chores at Plymouth colony?

Every family member was expected to perform a variety of daily chores: cooking, curing meat, drying fruit, spinning, weaving, mending, sewing, tapping shoes, repairing tools, making soap, churning butter, preparing seed for planting, hoeing, weeding, reaping crops, storing the harvest, chopping wood, feeding fires, carrying water, building and maintaining shelters for man and beast, caring for cows, goats, sheep, pigs, and chickens. The outdoor world was inviting at least eight months out of the year, offering an outlet that relieved family tensions. There was hunting in the forests for turkey, partridge, quail, and deer, and in the lowlands for ducks and geese. There was fishing in the ponds for perch, bass, and pickerel, and from a dory on the ocean for cod, haddock, and sole. Along the beach, clams, quahogs, scallops and oysters were to be gleaned. There was scant temptation to be idle or to indulge oneself since work was always to be performed in order to increase the security of the household.

Source: *The Faith Of The Pilgrims* by Robert M. Bartlett

PRACTICAL LEARNING

Building a home in the wilderness was daunting work, and everyone in the household was expected to contribute. Even young children were given simple chores to do, and by the age of six or seven—children could often be seen working alongside a parent in the home or out in the fields. Once each child reached an age of understanding, the education process began. A young boy typically learned how to hunt, mend fences, and plant crops with his father, while young girls learned skills such as spinning, cooking, and candle-making from their mother. Everyone shared the burden of daily household chores, and entire families worked together in the fields during the busy seasons of seedtime and harvest. Teaching children early on how to provide shelter, procure food, and maintain a home in the wilderness was essential for their survival. Every child needed to know how to become self-sufficient, and each task they learned was a vital means to an end.

The Pilgrims believed it was their responsibility to teach children how to be faithful Christians and productive members of society—that if you "train up a child in the way he should go; even when he is old he will not depart from it." (Proverbs 22:6) Relying on the Bible and practical, hands-on instruction—the Pilgrims educated their children in ways that may seem primitive compared to our modern systems of public education. "Yet for two hundred years in American history, from the mid-1600s to the mid-1800s, public schools as we know them today were virtually non-existent, and… the educational needs of America were met by the free market. In these two centuries, America produced several generations of highly skilled and literate men and women who laid the foundation for a nation dedicated to the principles of freedom and self-government."[137]

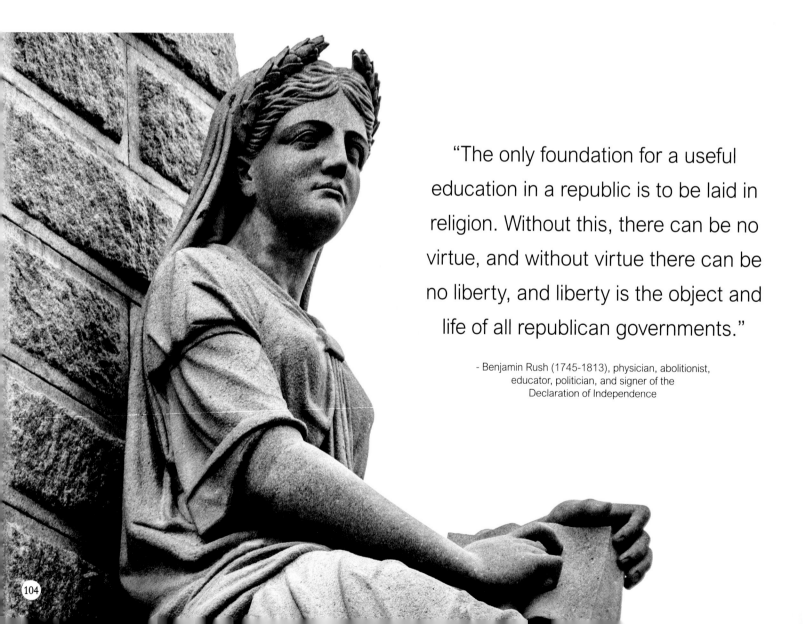

"The only foundation for a useful education in a republic is to be laid in religion. Without this, there can be no virtue, and without virtue there can be no liberty, and liberty is the object and life of all republican governments."

- Benjamin Rush (1745-1813), physician, abolitionist, educator, politician, and signer of the Declaration of Independence

HISTORICAL INFLUENCE

With the arrival of the Pilgrims at Plymouth Colony, the influence of Scripture in teaching literacy became embedded in America's educational roots. Although the Pilgrims used the Geneva Bible as their primary schoolbook, another essential resource was a book of worship called the *Ainsworth Psalter*. Commonly used in church worship, a Psalter compiled the Old Testament's Book of Psalms into a single volume for singing, reading, and devotions. In 1612, a Separatist pastor named Henry Ainsworth published his version of a Psalter in Amsterdam, which soon became a staple of Separatist church worship. Ainsworth's rhyming, metrical translation of the Psalms featured easy melodies while staying remarkably faithful to the original text of Scripture. Many early Pilgrims were accomplished singers, and the Ainsworth Psalter played a prominent role in the congregational-style worship observed in Plymouth colony. Along with the Bible, it was a vital resource to teach children how to read—a practice that continued well into the late 17th century.

ABOVE: *The Mainz Psalter was commissioned in 1457 by the Archbishop of Mainz, which is part of Germany today. Two versions were printed, each holding 143 and 175 leaves, respectively, with the more extended version designed for use in the diocese of Mainz. It has the distinction of being only the second major book to be printed in the West using movable type, the first being the Gutenberg Bible. Among several innovations, the Mainz Psalter was the first book to feature two type sizes, three colors of ink, decorative initials, and a publishing statement known as a colophon--which featured the date and location of publication. Only ten known copies remain today, although some vellum fragments have survived.*

Seventy years after the Pilgrims first landed in Plymouth, thousands of children across New England were learning how to read using a tiny book called The New England Primer. Considered the nation's first educational textbook, the New England Primer used Biblical themes and vivid illustrations to introduce spelling, reading, and grammar to generations of young children. Reminiscent of how early Pilgrim parents used the family Bible to teach children to read, the New England Primer offered reading material such as the Ten Commandments, a catechism, the Golden Rule, poetry, and prose to teach literacy. The world of reading opened to children as they learned, *"Be you to others kind and true, as you'd have others be to you,"* and *"Now I lay me down to sleep, I pray the Lord my soul to keep."* Employing Biblical themes of charity and virtue to educate children, the New England Primer was a formative learning tool in most early American households—second only to the Bible itself. It shaped the young lives of leaders such as John Adams, Benjamin Franklin, and John Hancock, and "our founding fathers were weaned on these beliefs."[138]

BELOW: *A copy of a 1764 New England Primer, printed and sold in Philadelphia by Benjamin Franklin and his business partner, David Hall.*

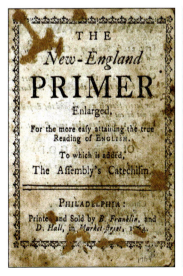

> Traditionally, organized education in the Western world was Church education. It could hardly be otherwise when the education of children was primarily study of the Word and the ways of God. Even in the Protestant countries, where there was a less close identification of Church and State, the basis of education was largely the Bible, and its chief purpose inculcation of piety. To the extent that the State intervened, it used its authority to further aims of the Church.
>
> - Justice Felix Frankfurter (1882-1965),
> U.S. Supreme Court Justice
>
> Source: https://www.law.cornell.edu/supremecourt/text/333/203

WISDOM

To the right of *Education's* pedestal, *Wisdom* is shown gazing up toward heaven for Divine insight as he stands amid learning tools such as books, an atlas, and the tablets of the Ten Commandments.

The Pilgrims were guided by men of great character, humility, and moral conviction as a church congregation. These rare leadership characteristics were matched in the lives of their female counterparts—the steely Pilgrim women who displayed an equal measure of courage and determination under pressure.

Although the colonists undoubtedly made mistakes, they were sincere people of faith who believed, "If any of you lacks wisdom, you should ask God, who gives generously to all without finding fault, and it will be given to you." (James 1:5) Through the uncommon wisdom of Pilgrim leaders such as John Robinson, John Carver, William Brewster, and William Bradford—the colonists were able to moderate conflict, persevere in the face of sickness and death, and in time, even achieve prosperity in Plymouth Colony.

Another Statue on the Forefathers' Monument

PLYMOUTH, Mass., October 7.—The great granite statue of Education was hoisted and safely placed upon the buttress of the Forefathers' Monument this morning. The statue occupies the southwest buttress, immediately in the rear of the statue of Morality. This completes the female statues. The remaining two statues—Law and Freedom—will be represented by male figures. Steps have been taken by members of the American Law Association to raise money to furnish the statue of Law.

PASTOR JOHN ROBINSON

Although he never set foot in Plymouth Colony, no one wielded more influence over the Pilgrims than their cherished pastor, John Robinson. Like a good father readying his children for an arduous journey, Robinson worked tirelessly to prepare his congregation for the difficult task of building a new colony in America. The voyage alone was perilous. Even if they safely reached land, Robinson knew it would be just one of many trials that could push the Pilgrims to the brink of civility. To prepare his church, he continually encouraged the Pilgrims to maintain the bonds of unity—and cautioned them against "the deadly plague of comfort."[139]

When financial circumstances forced the addition of outside passengers to their voyage, Robinson urged his members to be considerate of those who did not share their faith. When "Strangers" joined the trip, Robinson cautioned the church to be "watchful that we ourselves neither give, nor easily take, offense."[140] However, recognizing that strife was inevitable at some point—he urged the congregation to "diligently quench it with brotherly forbearance" for the sake of maintaining peace.[141] Pastor Robinson's acute influence is evident throughout the words of Mayflower Compact. Although he died before joining his beloved church in America, Robinson's legacy of faith, prudence, and wisdom remained a guiding force for the Pilgrims at Plymouth Colony.

ABOVE: *In 1914, Rev. John Robinson was featured on a $10,000 Federal Reserve Note, which became the highest denomination of US currency to circulate publicly. The front of the bill featured President Lincoln's Secretary of the Treasury, Salmon P. Chase. On the reverse, Robinson is shown from the iconic work, "Embarkation of the Pilgrims," which is displayed at the U.S. Capitol rotunda in Washington, D.C..*

ELDER WILLIAM BREWSTER

When Pastor Robinson decided to remain behind and care for the rest of the congregation in Leiden, he appointed Elder William Brewster as the spiritual leader over the departing Pilgrims. At Plymouth Colony, Elder Brewster faithfully delivered two sermons at church every Sunday for several years before a formal minister arrived to replace him.

ABOVE: *In his 1876 painting, "Pilgrims Going To Church," American artist George Henry Boughton depicts the Pilgrim's weekly walk to their meeting house every Sunday for worship. In front, Elder William Brewster leads the Pilgrim assembly to church.*

Affable and kind, Elder Brewster was deeply loved by the congregation. His death was a tremendous loss for the colony when he passed away at seventy-seven. Brewster also profoundly impacted young William Bradford, who lost his father as a boy. After spending decades studying together and working alongside each church ministry—their relationship became that of a father and son. Upon his death, Bradford eulogized Brewster as "wise and discreet and well spoken… of a very cheerful spirit, very sociable and pleasant amongst his friends, of an humble and modest mind, of a peaceable disposition… inoffensive and innocent in his life and conversation, which gained him the love" of all who knew him.[142] Hand-picked by Pastor Robinson for his mature faith and steady leadership, Brewster led the Pilgrims through countless trials and his life "was a product of the Pilgrim ethics."[143]

GOVERNOR JOHN CARVER

John Carver was a trusted deacon in the church at Leiden and a man known for his integrity and prudent leadership skills. When the congregation decided to leave Holland for America, Carver was instrumental in arranging the voyage. Highly regarded by his peers, Carver was the obvious choice to serve as Plymouth's first governor—a distinction that made him "the first colonial governor in the New World, probably the first in history, to be named by the colonists themselves and chosen by democratic means in a free election."[144] As governor, Carver displayed great wisdom and deference in his exchanges with Chief Massasoit. His respectful displays of diplomacy helped foster a peace treaty with the Wampanoags that would endure for over fifty years.

In the spring of 1621, Carver's time in office was unexpectedly cut short. One afternoon, while out "working in the fields with the other settlers, setting the pattern of democratic leadership,"

ABOVE: *In the marble panel, "Treaty with Massasoit," Gov. Carver is shown signing the peace treaty with Chief Massasoit, the Grand Sachem of the Wampanoags.*

Carver collapsed and later died from sunstroke.[145] The Pilgrims grieved the loss of this faithful deacon and steadfast friend, and the colony's first governor was memorialized as "a leader of singular piety… rare for humility."[146] Thirty-one-year-old William Bradford was elected to replace Carver, making him Plymouth's second—and in time, longest-serving governor. This unexpected promotion would propel Bradford into the annals of history and establish him arguably as Plymouth's wisest, most enduring leader.

GOVERNOR WILLIAM BRADFORD

Characterized as "a genuine Christian and a consummate politician," William Bradford was reluctant to assume the role of the colony's governor after Carver's death.[147] Once in office, however, he proved himself to be "talented and indefatigable, passionately devoted to the welfare of New Plimoth."[148] As a leader, Bradford was the living embodiment of the wise proverb, "When the righteous are in authority, the people rejoice." (Proverbs 29:2) Time and again, the people of Plymouth handily re-elected Bradford as their governor. At times he even refused the office to allow others to serve, a gesture which likely stemmed from his disdain for England's fixed, monarchial rule.

An astute observer of both the Bible and human nature, Bradford "worked well with men because he loved and honored them as God's creatures, the end and purpose of the divine scheme."[149] Bradford was an essential leader in church and government and exemplified the Pilgrim way of life. To many historians, Bradford *was* the colony. His compelling journals, which were famously compiled and published in the book, *Of Plymouth Plantation,* have been described as "a remarkable work by a man who himself was something of a marvel."[150] In *Bradford of Plymouth,* author Bradford Smith asserts: "Bradford was unquestionably the greatest of the Pilgrims, one of the greatest figures of seventeenth century New England— indeed, of our whole colonial period."[151]

LEFT: *A statue of Governor Bradford stands in front of Pilgrim Memorial State Park at the Plymouth waterfront near the Mayflower II, a replica of the ship which brought the Pilgrims from England.*

YOUTH

On the left side of *Education's* pedestal, *Youth* is depicted by the image of a mother gazing down upon her child. Holding a book in one hand, the mother clasps her son's hand to symbolize their connection as teacher and student. Looking up to his mother for guidance, the child can be seen holding a scroll of paper to indicate his active role in learning. Together, they represent the crucial role of parents in educating their children and imparting knowledge and wisdom to the next generation.

After building a new life at Plymouth Colony, when the Pilgrims looked back on their time in Holland, they recalled "how hard the country was where we lived, how many spent their estate in it … how unable we were to give such good education to our children as we received."[152] In Leiden, the Pilgrims worked long hours outside the home to make ends meet. Parents felt deprived of the necessary time to educate their children and cultivate a healthy family life. They hoped that America would offer greater opportunities to educate and influence their children—and it did.

At Plymouth Colony, "young and old were together most of the time. The family was the center for teaching morality… and building Christian character. Youth were admonished and guided, and the unruly were disciplined… and a sustaining faith was created and rooted in the spiritual values of the Bible."[153] While both parents played an important role in raising and training children, women were the primary educators of the home.

ABOVE/LEFT: *Youth is symbolized in the depiction of two generations, a mother and her child, and situated on the left of Education's seated pedestal.*

"…how hard the country was where we lived, how many spent their estate in it… how unable we were to give such good education to our children as we received."

THE INFLUENCE OF WOMEN

The vital role of women at Plymouth Colony cannot be overstated. As wives, mothers, educators, and nurturers—Pilgrim women proved themselves to be instrumental in the colony's success. Many historians believe that the Pilgrims avoided many of the perils of Jamestown's all-male settlement precisely because Plymouth Colony included women and children. At Plymouth, men were surrounded by the comforts of family and faith and shared the difficult work of building a new settlement with their female counterparts. It can easily be argued that without the presence of strong, capable Pilgrim women in the New England wilderness— the story of Plymouth Colony might have unfolded quite differently.

During their first winter at Plymouth, a brutal epidemic wiped out entire families at once. Of the eighteen wives who crossed the Atlantic on the Mayflower—only four survived. Sickness was rampant among the settlers, and women sacrificed themselves to nurse sick, suffering children back to health. Because of their selfless acts, younger boys and girls had a much higher survival rate. The few mothers who did survive that winter took newly orphaned children into their homes to be raised as their own. Although the colony was decimated by disease during its first year, "the fifty-one survivors were able to endure in large measure because they were part of firmly knit households."[154] As wives, mothers, nurses, teachers, and wilderness settlers—the pioneering women of Plymouth Colony held the settlement together with their love, faith, resiliency, and steely strength. Their contributions to the Pilgrim legacy are incalculable, and these trail-blazing women "form an assemblage equal in full measure to the Pilgrim fathers."[155]

ABOVE/LEFT/RIGHT: *The Pilgrim Mother Fountain on Water Street in Plymouth was a gift from the Daughters of the American Revolution in 1921 to commemorate the Tercentenary Celebration. German-American sculptor Carl Paul Jennewein (1890-1978) was chosen to create the fountain to honor the Pilgrim mothers of Plymouth Colony. Behind the statue, the individual names of the Pilgrim women are etched in stone, and their lives are memorialized with the following tribute (shown right):*

THEY BROUGHT UP THEIR FAMILIES IN STURDY VIRTUE AND A LIVING FAITH IN GOD WITHOUT WHICH NATIONS PERISH

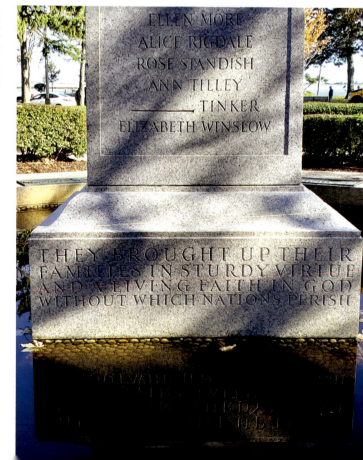

> As wives, mothers, nurses, teachers, and wilderness settlers—the pioneering women of Plymouth Colony held the settlement together with their love, faith, resiliency, and steely strength. Their contributions to the Pilgrim legacy are incalculable, and these trail-blazing women 'form an assemblage equal in full measure to the Pilgrim fathers.'

"The most important business in this Nation—or any other nation, for that matter—is raising and training children. If those children have the proper environment at home, and educationally... very, very few of them ever turn out wrong. I don't think we put enough stress on the necessity of implanting in the child's mind the moral code under which we live. The fundamental basis of this Nation's law was given to Moses on the Mount. The fundamental basis of our Bill of Rights comes from the teachings which we get from Exodus and St. Matthew, from Isaiah and St. Paul. I don't think we emphasize that enough these days. If we don't have the proper fundamental moral background, we will finally wind up with a totalitarian government which does not believe in rights for anybody except the state."

- Harry S. Truman (1884-1972),
33rd President of the United States

MARBLE BAS-RELIEF PANEL: SIGNING OF THE MAYFLOWER COMPACT

In establishing their new settlement, the Pilgrims created a civic order for government in the best way they knew—they modeled it after their practice of self-government as a church. Back home in England, the intertwined powers of church and state functioned in a "top-down" manner. The king or queen held ultimate authority as the Head of State and Supreme Head of the Church. The Church of England was the official church denomination of the state—and every citizen was required to attend regardless of what they believed. As the principal leader of the church, the Archbishop wielded complete authority over all local churches—and was frequently a political mouthpiece for the monarchy. By contrast, the Pilgrims believed the church was meant to be a voluntary gathering of those who demonstrated sincere faith and a genuine desire to worship God. As Separatists, they rejected the idea of forced church attendance—insisting that "ungodly, profane persons could not create a true church."156 They rejected the tyrannical abuse of church officials—and how "a semi-political church inspector, called a bishop, could imprison or hang you" without warning or just cause.[157] In stark contrast to the entrenched power structures of the state-run Church of England, the Pilgrim congregations at Scrooby and Leiden "chose their minister, their officers, and their organization, and ran the enterprise free from outside state or ecclesiastical control."[158]

In this manner, the Pilgrims governed their church from a "downward up" model. The Lord Jesus Christ was King, and Holy Scripture—God's declared, Sovereign will—held final authority in all matters of faith. Each church was a free gathering of sincere believers, and every congregation elected its leaders. As the primary teacher of the congregation, the pastor worked with church-appointed elders and deacons to serve the church's members—not rule over them. This style of Congregational church government would become a template for civic affairs at Plymouth Colony. Guided by the Mayflower Compact, the Pilgrims pioneered the idea of self-government based on the expressed will of the people—planting the seeds of freedom for what would later become the United States of America.

As the story goes, when John Adams drafted the Massachusetts State Constitution in 1779, he drew great inspiration from early documents such as the Magna Carta and the Mayflower Compact. From her first words of independence to the preamble of her oldest state constitution—see if you detect the influence of the Pilgrim forefathers on America's founding ideals.

MAYFLOWER COMPACT
November 21, 1620

In the name of God, Amen. Having undertaken, for the Glory of God, and advancements of the Christian faith, and the honor of our King and Country, a voyage to plant the first colony in the Northern parts of Virginia; do by these presents, solemnly and mutually, in the presence of God, and one another; covenant and combine ourselves together into a civil body politic; for our better ordering, and preservation and furtherance of the ends aforesaid; and by virtue hereof to enact, constitute, and frame, such just and equal laws, ordinances, acts, constitutions, and offices, from time to time, as shall be thought most meet and convenient for the general good of the colony; unto which we promise all due submission and obedience.

DECLARATION OF INDEPENDENCE
July 4, 1776

When in the Course of human events, it becomes necessary for one people to dissolve the political bands which have connected them with another, and to assume among the powers of the earth, the separate and equal station to which the Laws of Nature and of Nature's God entitle them, a decent respect to the opinions of mankind requires that they should declare the causes which impel them to the separation.

We hold these truths to be self-evident, that all men are created equal, that they are endowed by their Creator with certain unalienable Rights, that among these are Life, Liberty and the pursuit of Happiness. That to secure these rights, Governments are instituted among Men, deriving their just powers from the consent of the governed— That whenever any Form of Government becomes destructive of these ends, it is the Right of the People to alter or to abolish it, and to institute new Government, laying its foundation on such principles and organizing its powers in such form, as to them shall seem most likely to effect their Safety and Happiness.

MASSACHUSETTS STATE CONSTITUTION
October 25, 1780

The end of the institution, maintenance, and administration of government, is to secure the existence of the body politic, to protect it, and to furnish the individuals who compose it with the power of enjoying in safety and tranquility their natural rights, and the blessings of life: and whenever these great objects are not obtained, the people have a right to alter the government, and to take measures necessary for their safety, prosperity and happiness.

The body politic is formed by a voluntary association of individuals: it is a social compact, by which the whole people covenants with each citizen, and each citizen with the whole people, that all shall be governed by certain laws for the common good. It is the duty of the people, therefore, in framing a constitution of government, to provide for an equitable mode of making laws, as well as for an impartial interpretation, and a faithful execution of them; that every man may, at all times, find his security in them.

We, therefore, the people of Massachusetts, acknowledging, with grateful hearts, the goodness of the great Legislator of the universe, in affording us, in the course of His providence, an opportunity, deliberately and peaceably, without fraud, violence or surprise, of entering into an original, explicit, and solemn compact with each other; and of forming a new constitution of civil government, for ourselves and posterity; and devoutly imploring His direction in so interesting a design, do agree upon, ordain and establish the following Declaration of Rights, and Frame of Government, as the Constitution of the Commonwealth of Massachusetts.

In large measure, their importance lies in the example they continue to afford of courage in the face of danger, resourcefulness in the face of difficulty, and fortitude in the face of adversity. In spiritual quality, the Pilgrim leaders were second to none in the New World, and in many respects, as Henry Adams said of the great Virginians at the close of the 18th century, they were "equal to any standard of excellence known to history. Their range was narrow, but within it they were supreme." At the same time, it must be recognized that Plymouth Colony made several important contributions to American legal institutions, not the least of which was an early articulation of the ideal that finds expression in the famous language of the Constitution of Massachusetts— "a government of laws and not of men."

Source: *The Legal Heritage Of Plymouth Colony* by George L. Haskins

"Liberty cannot be established without morality, nor without faith."

- Alexis de Tocqueville (1805-1859), French diplomat, historian, political scientist, and author of *"Democracy in America"*

LIBERTY

INSTALLED:
October 1888

ORDER:
Liberty (initially called *Freedom*) was the fourth of the five allegorical figures to be set in place.

COST:
$13,500

SPONSOR:
The United States Congress appropriated $15,000 to produce *Liberty* and the lower bas-relief panel *Pilgrim Landing*. From this grant, $13,500 was used, and the balance was applied to fund the figure of *Law* and the corresponding marble bas-relief panel *Treaty with Massasoit*.

DESIGNER:
Working from the original drawings of Hammatt Billings (1818-74), *Liberty* was designed by sculptor J.H. Mahoney (1855-1919).

HEIGHT:
Approximately 15 ft.

WEIGHT:
Approximately 25 tons, cut from a single block.

LOWER MARBLE BAS-RELIEF PANEL:
Pilgrim Landing was modeled by sculptor J.H. Mahoney (1855-1919), and sponsored by the United States Congress.

Undoubtedly the monument's most complex and captivating figure, *Liberty* is revealed as the culmination of all Pilgrim virtues. Seated in triumph as a conquering hero, *Liberty* is shown draped in the victor's prize of a slain lion's pelt. In one hand, he cradles a sword, and in the other, he holds the broken chains of his captivity. In this heroic depiction, *Liberty* symbolizes freedom from all tyranny and oppression.

RELIGIOUS FREEDOM

The Pilgrims established several kinds of freedom at Plymouth Colony, but their foundational achievement was religious freedom—which set the stage for all other liberties. After escaping England's ruthless religious persecution, the Pilgrims sought refuge in Holland. But although they could practice their faith openly in Leiden, threats from England still hung in the air.

Even across the Atlantic, Separatists were still hunted down and harassed. Elder William Brewster operated a printing press in Leiden. When Brewster published books deemed critical of King James—his press was seized, and he was thrown in jail. After briefly releasing Brewster due to sickness, he went into hiding for almost a year to evade the English authorities. Many surmise his next public appearance was boarding the *Mayflower* for the Pilgrim's voyage to America.

ABOVE: *Liberty was the fourth of the five allegorical figures to be set in place.*

The Pilgrims also struggled to maintain a Biblical lifestyle in Holland's decadent culture. "While the relaxed, liberal attitude typical of Dutch culture allowed for greater religious tolerance than was found in England… it also produced a general lack of personal discipline and a casual attitude toward Bible-based morality."[159] Parents stood heartbroken as children became enticed and corrupted by the "the great licentiousness of the young people of the country."[160] For the Pilgrims, freedom was a gift from God—not a license for selfish pursuits: "You, my brothers and sisters, were called to be free. But do not use your freedom to indulge the flesh; rather, serve one another humbly in love." (Galatians 5:13) In the new settlement, the Pilgrims were free to shape their own culture according to the tenants of their faith. Friendly and welcoming by nature, Bradford wrote of their eagerness to "show a rare example of brotherly love and Christian care" to all who later joined the colony.[161] In stark proof of this, "during the first three decades of Plymouth Colony, no stranger was turned away and the plantation endeavored to extend hospitality to those who came seeking a haven."[162]

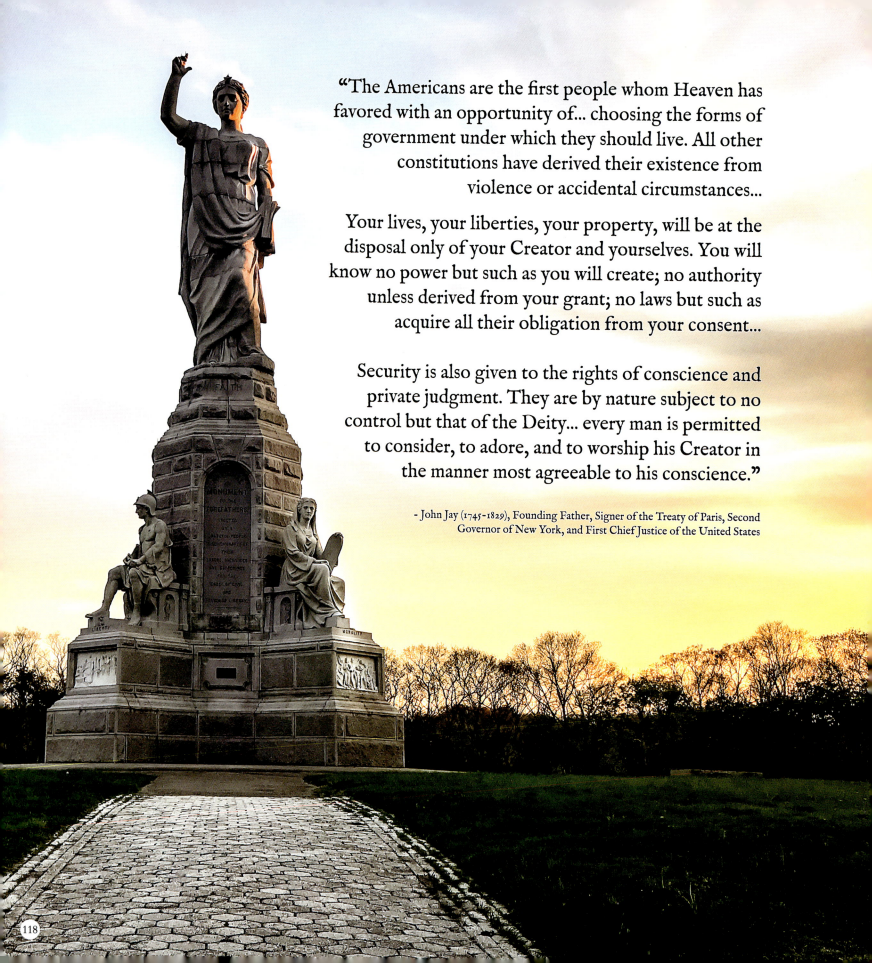

"The Americans are the first people whom Heaven has favored with an opportunity of... choosing the forms of government under which they should live. All other constitutions have derived their existence from violence or accidental circumstances...

Your lives, your liberties, your property, will be at the disposal only of your Creator and yourselves. You will know no power but such as you will create; no authority unless derived from your grant; no laws but such as acquire all their obligation from your consent...

Security is also given to the rights of conscience and private judgment. They are by nature subject to no control but that of the Deity... every man is permitted to consider, to adore, and to worship his Creator in the manner most agreeable to his conscience."

- John Jay (1745-1829), Founding Father, Signer of the Treaty of Paris, Second Governor of New York, and First Chief Justice of the United States

ECONOMIC FREEDOM

After a difficult start, the colony would also achieve economic freedom. To finance their voyage to America, the Pilgrims struck a deal with London investors known as the Merchant Adventurers. In return for funding their endeavor, the Pilgrims agreed to share future profits from the colony with the Adventurers until their debt was paid. "On arrival in Plymouth the settlers faced the superhuman task of building homes, planting crops, and starting debt payments."[163]

To their dismay, nothing went to plan. The colonists were decimated by sickness during their first winter at Plymouth. It was a struggle to feed themselves, let alone repay any debt. Even worse, the first two ships the Pilgrims sent to London filled with goods toward repayment were hijacked by pirates—all their hard work was lost. It was a dispiriting time.

> I answer...
> that God in His wisdom
> saw that another plan of life
> was fitter for them.

For the first three years, Plymouth Colony operated as a communal economy while the colonists worked to fulfill the terms of their contract with the Adventurers. But along with the practice of collective farming came a disparity of workload—some colonists labored long and hard, while others contributed less. Regardless of individual effort, the outcome was always the same. It wasn't long before many became resentful.

"The failure of this experiment of communal service, which was tried for several years, and by good and honest men, proves the emptiness of the theory of Plato and other ancients, applauded by some of later times, that the taking away of private property, and the possession of it in community by a commonwealth, would make a state happy and flourishing; as if they were wiser than God. For in this instance, community of property (so far as it went) was found to breed much confusion and discontent, and retard much employment which would have been to the general benefit and comfort."

– Governor William Bradford

According to Bradford, "The young men who were most able and fit for service objected to being forced to spend their time and strength in working for other men's wives and children, without any recompense. The strong man or the resourceful man had no more share of food, clothes, etc., than the weak man who was not able to do a quarter the other could. This was thought injustice. As for men's wives who were obliged to do service for other men… many husbands would not brook it."[164] He continued, saying: "Let none argue that this is due to human failing, rather than to this communistic plan of life in itself. I answer, seeing that all men have this failing in them, that God in His wisdom saw that another plan of life was fitter for them."[165]

And with that, Governor Bradford ordered a return to private enterprise. "The governor, with the advice of the chief among them, allowed each man to plant corn for his own household, and to trust to themselves for that. Every family was assigned a parcel of land, according to the proportion of their number… all children being included under some family. This was very successful. It made all hands very industrious, so that much more corn was planted than otherwise would have been. The women now went willingly into the field, and took their little ones with them to plant corn, while before they would allege weakness and inability; and to have compelled them would have been thought great tyranny and oppression."[166]

> If there had been no Aptuxet Trading Post, we would have no monument to the origin of the free economy practiced by the Pilgrims today. The original foundation upon which the Trading Post was constructed was partially excavated in 1852 but then completed beginning in 1926. The restored building on its original foundation is probably the oldest Pilgrim foundation still visible today.
>
> Source: Dr. Paul Jehle, Plymouth Rock Foundation

BELOW: *A modern replica of the 1627 Aptuxet Trading Post located in Bourne, Massachusetts, built by the Pilgrims to facilitate trade with the local Wampanoag people and traveling Dutch traders.*

1627 Aptuxet Trading Post

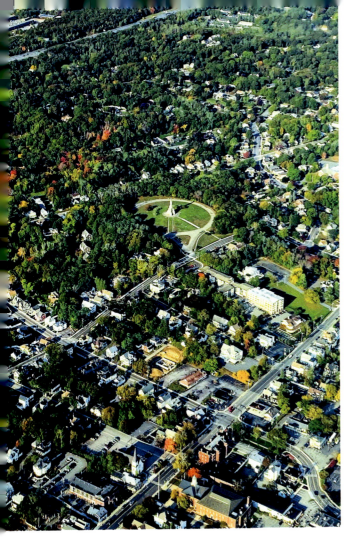

ABOVE: *A view of the monument from a plane flying 2000 feet above ground.*

In their first year at Plymouth, the Pilgrims gathered in a meager harvest from 26 acres of shared agriculture—and struggled to survive. Under this same shared system, the colony increased its production to 60 acres in the second year. By the third year, after they switched from communal living to private enterprise—the colonists planted an astounding 184 acres. It was a turning point for the colony, and scarcity would never be a concern again. Under this capitalist model, the Pilgrims thrived. Biographer Bradford Smith, author of *Bradford of Plymouth,* observes: "There is nothing more instructive in our history than the changes that took place in this little communist village as it shaped itself to become, unknowingly, the pattern for a great democracy."[167]

But as new settlers joined the colony in the ensuing years, it complicated the original terms of the Pilgrim's contract with the Merchant Adventurers. To settle Plymouth's nagging debt, several leaders stepped forward to underwrite the colony's loan balance personally. Eight men signed on as personal guarantors, including William Brewster, William Bradford, Myles Standish, Isaac Allerton, John Alden, John Howland, Edward Winslow, and Thomas Prence. "They might have reneged on the note and it would have been impossible for the Adventurers to collect. But they stood behind their promise and their signatures. The Pilgrim ethics confronted a rigorous test and stood firm. The bulk of the debt was paid in 1645; the final claim of one Adventurer was met in 1648. To conclude this settlement Winslow and Prence sold their own houses and other 'undertakers' sold some of their land."[168] Almost thirty years after establishing their new settlement, the Pilgrims had finally achieved economic liberty at Plymouth Colony.

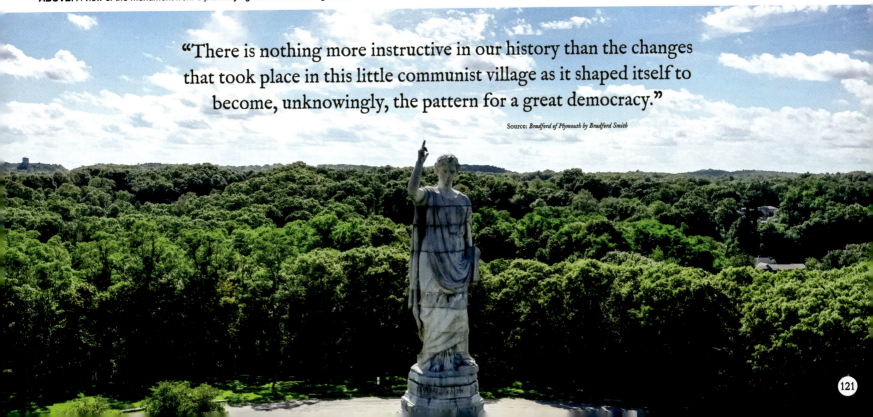

"There is nothing more instructive in our history than the changes that took place in this little communist village as it shaped itself to become, unknowingly, the pattern for a great democracy."

Source: *Bradford of Plymouth by Bradford Smith*

ABOVE: In "Pilgrim Overboard," marine artist Mike Haywood shows John Howland desperately clutching the Mayflower's trailing rope.

"Once, as they thus lay at hull in a terrible storm, a strong young man, called John Howland, coming on deck was thrown into the sea; but it pleased God that he caught hold of the top-sail halliards which hung overboard and ran out at length; but he kept his hold, though he was several fathoms under water, till he was hauled up by the rope and then with a boat-hook helped into the ship and saved; and though he was somewhat ill from it he lived many years and became a profitable member both of the church and commonwealth."

Source: Bradford's History of the Plymouth Settlement, 1608-1650

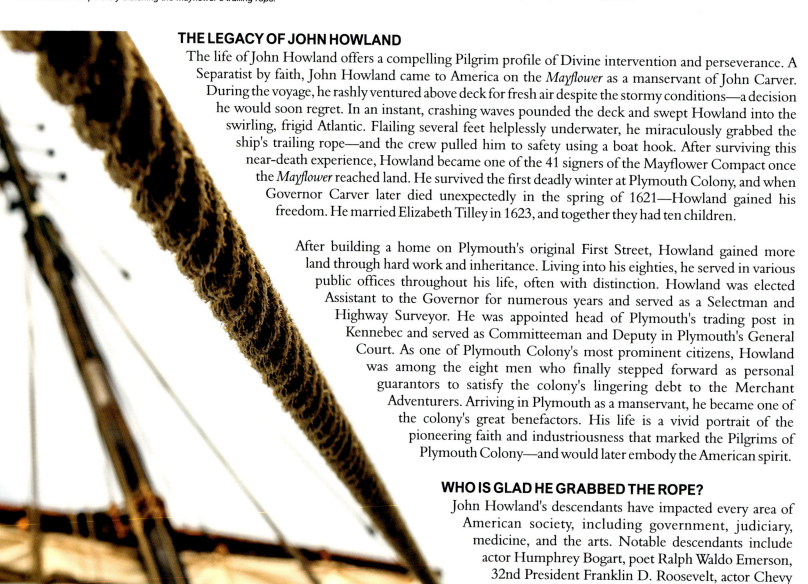

THE LEGACY OF JOHN HOWLAND

The life of John Howland offers a compelling Pilgrim profile of Divine intervention and perseverance. A Separatist by faith, John Howland came to America on the *Mayflower* as a manservant of John Carver. During the voyage, he rashly ventured above deck for fresh air despite the stormy conditions—a decision he would soon regret. In an instant, crashing waves pounded the deck and swept Howland into the swirling, frigid Atlantic. Flailing several feet helplessly underwater, he miraculously grabbed the ship's trailing rope—and the crew pulled him to safety using a boat hook. After surviving this near-death experience, Howland became one of the 41 signers of the Mayflower Compact once the *Mayflower* reached land. He survived the first deadly winter at Plymouth Colony, and when Governor Carver later died unexpectedly in the spring of 1621—Howland gained his freedom. He married Elizabeth Tilley in 1623, and together they had ten children.

After building a home on Plymouth's original First Street, Howland gained more land through hard work and inheritance. Living into his eighties, he served in various public offices throughout his life, often with distinction. Howland was elected Assistant to the Governor for numerous years and served as a Selectman and Highway Surveyor. He was appointed head of Plymouth's trading post in Kennebec and served as Committeeman and Deputy in Plymouth's General Court. As one of Plymouth Colony's most prominent citizens, Howland was among the eight men who finally stepped forward as personal guarantors to satisfy the colony's lingering debt to the Merchant Adventurers. Arriving in Plymouth as a manservant, he became one of the colony's great benefactors. His life is a vivid portrait of the pioneering faith and industriousness that marked the Pilgrims of Plymouth Colony—and would later embody the American spirit.

WHO IS GLAD HE GRABBED THE ROPE?

John Howland's descendants have impacted every area of American society, including government, judiciary, medicine, and the arts. Notable descendants include actor Humphrey Bogart, poet Ralph Waldo Emerson, 32nd President Franklin D. Roosevelt, actor Chevy Chase, singer Mary Chapin Carpenter, author Jane Austin, Dr. Benjamin Spock, Supreme Court Justice Robert Jackson, 41st President George H.W. Bush, Governor Sarah Palin, and Senator Sam Ervin.

Source: The Pilgrim John Howland Society

ABOVE: *The early settlement of Plymouth Colony has been re-created as one of several interactive exhibits offered by the Plimoth-Patuxet Museum in Plymouth, Massachusetts.*

A Tale of Two Colonies

The first two permanent settlements in early America offer a fascinating contrast in ideologies and outcomes. While the Jamestown settlement in Virginia was essentially a continuation of the European model of its day, the Pilgrims and Puritans who settled in Massachusetts chartered a new path of self-government, civic and religious freedom, and capitalistic, free-market trade.

JAMESTOWN COLONY

1. Considered all land the property of the king.
2. Colonists worked for the monarchy in a socialistic economy; no private property was allowed.
3. Limited vocational training or experience in the trades; a background of monarchial rule, elitism, and socialism bred a poor work ethic.
4. Most were professing Christians in the state-sponsored Anglican Church, but few had personal knowledge of Scripture.
5. Continued England's civil system of monarchial rule.
6. Continued England's ethnic and class distinctions.
7. Rejected equality; introduced the common practice of "chattel" slavery from Europe.
8. When confronted with hardship and death, many of the colonists became desperate, debased, and practiced cannibalism.

PLYMOUTH COLONY

1. Purchased land from the natives; created a registry of deeds to promote fair dealings.
2. After the failure of socialism, the Pilgrims enacted capitalism; they encouraged private property and instituted free-market trade.
3. Skilled tradesmen and laborers; years of hard labor in Holland had produced a strong work ethic.
4. Evangelistic Christians who studied Scripture for themselves; endeavored to follow God's laws.
5. Created civil order based on Biblical laws.
6. Rejected British class distinctions.
7. Practiced equality; rejected slavery and passed laws against "manstealing" on Biblical grounds.
8. When confronted with hardship and death, the colonists selflessly served one another, and sought God through fasting and prayer.

Source: *The American Story* by David Barton and Tim Barton

> The Pilgrims believed that liberty came from God, not the state. At Plymouth Colony, they articulated the role of government as being vested with certain powers, not to *grant* freedom—but to *protect* it.

CONSTITUTIONAL FREEDOM

In 1636, the Pilgrims established constitutional liberty by forming the Pilgrim Code of Law. Building on the precepts of the Mayflower Compact, the 1636 Pilgrim Code of Law cemented the rights of all citizens in the first basic constitution of the New World. For over two centuries in the United States, Americans have lived with the expectation of protected freedoms, but for these early colonists—the concept was groundbreaking.

As Noah Webster, early textbook pioneer and "Father of American Scholarship and Education," wrote: "The Puritans who planted the first colonies in New England, established institutions on republican principles. They founded governments on the principle that the people are the sources of power; the representatives being elected annually, and of course responsible to their constituents. And especially they made early provisions for schools for diffusing knowledge among all the members of their communities, that the people might learn their rights and their duties. Their liberal and wise institutions, which were then novelties in the world, have been the foundation of our republican governments."[169]

The Pilgrims believed that liberty came from God, not the state. At Plymouth Colony, they articulated the role of government as being vested with certain powers, not to *grant* freedom—but to *protect* it. America's Founding Fathers shared this fundamental principle of liberty, declaring: "We hold these truths to be self-evident, that all men are created equal, that they are endowed by their Creator with certain unalienable Rights, that among these are Life, Liberty and the pursuit of Happiness. That to secure these rights, Governments are instituted among Men, deriving their just powers from the consent of the governed."[170] These undeniable truths paved the way for later constitutional amendments that would abolish the sin of slavery, secure the right of every citizen to vote, and continue America on her historical path to form *"a more perfect union."*

Over 400 years ago, the Pilgrims relied on principles of *Faith, Morality, Law, Education,* and *Liberty* to establish the remarkable practice of self-government at Plymouth Colony. Their legacy formed the bedrock of American independence in 1776 and, if preserved—will ensure her freedom and prosperity for generations to come.

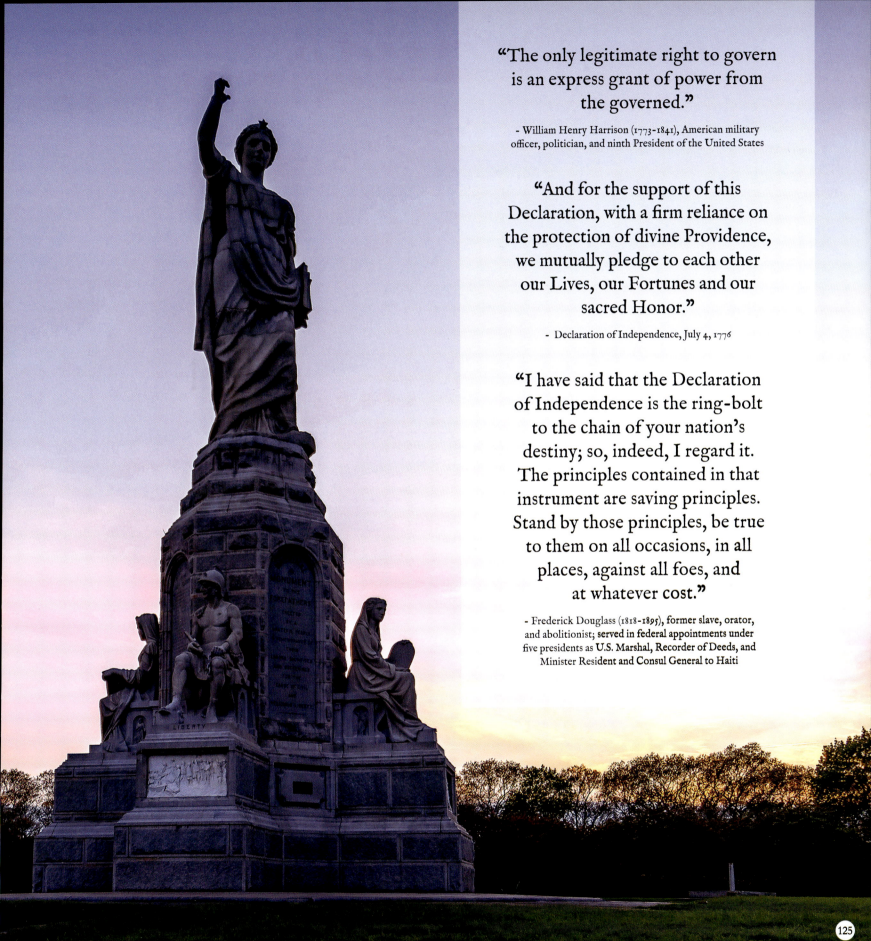

> "The only legitimate right to govern is an express grant of power from the governed."
>
> - William Henry Harrison (1773-1841), American military officer, politician, and ninth President of the United States

> "And for the support of this Declaration, with a firm reliance on the protection of divine Providence, we mutually pledge to each other our Lives, our Fortunes and our sacred Honor."
>
> - Declaration of Independence, July 4, 1776

> "I have said that the Declaration of Independence is the ring-bolt to the chain of your nation's destiny; so, indeed, I regard it. The principles contained in that instrument are saving principles. Stand by those principles, be true to them on all occasions, in all places, against all foes, and at whatever cost."
>
> - Frederick Douglass (1818-1895), former slave, orator, and abolitionist; served in federal appointments under five presidents as U.S. Marshal, Recorder of Deeds, and Minister Resident and Consul General to Haiti

HELMET

Depicted in the classic style of a Greek soldier, *Liberty* wears the crest of a high-ranking officer. His helmet is embellished with a sunrise to symbolize Divine guidance, and the "tender mercy of our God, by which the rising sun will come to us from heaven to shine on those living in darkness… to guide our feet into the path of peace." (Luke 1:78-79) Here, the sunrise represents the dawn of peace and freedom at Plymouth Colony, to which William Bradford proclaimed, "let the glorious name of Jehovah have all the praise."[171]

ABOVE: *Greek soldiers in the Greco-Persion Wars display various military costume.*

SWORD

Although *Liberty* is armed with a sword, his weapon is sheathed in a protected, watchful position. After landing in Plymouth, the Pilgrims welcomed a peace alliance with the Wampanoag tribe and viewed conflict as a defensive act to guard the colony. When Governor Carver unexpectedly died shortly after signing the *Pilgrim-Wampanoag Peace Treaty,* newly elected Governor Bradford dispatched diplomatic teams to visit Chief Massasoit and reinforce their desire for peace. Bradford wisely repeated this diplomatic gesture with several "other tribes in the region, and he also reimbursed the Nausets for the corn that the Pilgrims had taken from them during their first days ashore."[172] The Pilgrims were greatly aided by their friendship with Squanto and worked earnestly to build alliances throughout the region that would "provide for peace with all men."[173]

"Those who would give up essential liberty, to purchase a little temporary safety, deserve neither liberty nor safety."

- Benjamin Franklin (1706-1790), inventor, publisher, scientist, and the only founding father to sign all four documents that were essential in forming the United States: the 1776 Declaration of Independence, the 1778 Treaty of Alliance with France, the 1783 Treaty of Paris which established peace with Great Britain, and the 1787 United States Constitution

DRAPED IN A LION PELT

Liberty is shown draped in a lion's pelt, and this dramatic imagery holds dual meaning. Firstly, the lion is representative of England. The use of a lion in royal seals and standards began under King Henry I (1068-1135) and continued in various iterations until the reign of King Richard I (1157-1199), also known as *"Richard the Lionheart."* King Richard established three golden lions on a scarlet red background to symbolize the English throne, and monarchs have used this iconic image on the Royal Coat of Arms to the present day. In Scripture, a lion is also symbolic of adversity. In the New Testament, the Apostle Peter urged his fellow believers to "Be alert and of sober mind. Your enemy the devil prowls around like a roaring lion looking for someone to devour." (1 Peter 5:8) Clothed in the pelt of a slain lion, *Liberty* announces the defeat of his mortal enemy—and signals an end to the religious tyranny that tormented the Pilgrims in England.

RIGHT: *The Royal Arms of England as depicted in stained glass at King's College, Cambridge, England.*

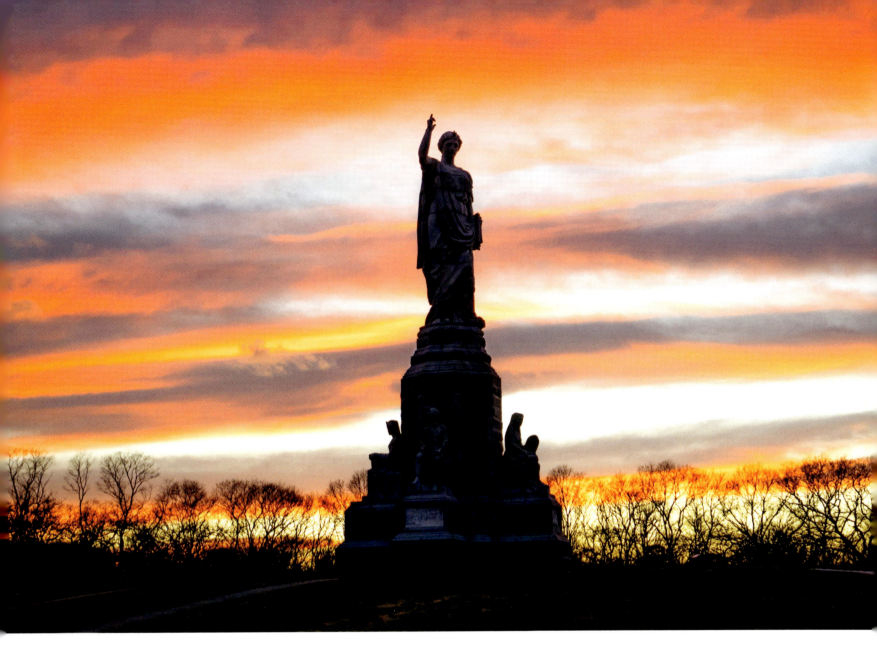

"Across American history, there have been countless fascinating stories of both the brave and the cowardly; of heroes and villains, of atrocities, corruption, and greed as well as self-sacrifice, honor and redemption. Our story is not one of a perfect people, but it is a compelling account of people seeking religious and civil freedom, escaping oppression, pursuing opportunity, and often joining hands with diverse people to achieve common goals."

Source: *The American Story* by David Barton and Tim Barton

BROKEN CHAINS

In his hands, *Liberty* holds the broken chains of his oppression. Traces of these chains can also be seen at his feet, in the imagery of the Psalmist who wrote, "He brought them out of darkness, the utter darkness, and broke away their chains." (Psalm 107:14)

In 17th century England, "the prisons of London were crammed with innocent people whose only crime was the sincerity of their Christian faith. Without benefit of habeas corpus, they had been thrown into jail by any bishop who suspected their nonconformity."[174] Separatists were routinely rooted out by government spies, or worse—betrayed by those closest to them, such as family members or friends.

Once captured, many were thrown into prisons "so foul, so disease-ridden, that few could survive an extended stay. With nothing but filthy straw to lie on, with no provision for human waste, no heat, and indifferent or positively rotten food, the strongest man soon succumbed."[175] Here, *Liberty*'s broken chains represent the overthrow of England's religious tyranny, where "non-conformists" were jailed for treason and often executed for their beliefs.

> It was not even necessary to commit an overt act of separation from the Church of England to be severely punished. George Cotton, for hearing a portion of Scripture read in a friend's house, was thrown into prison for twenty-seven months without being brought to trial. If a man's family should refuse to attend church, he could be thrown into jail merely for harboring his own kin. In order to convict imprisoned Separatist preachers, the bishops were willing to go beyond the bounds of fair play. In London, forty-two preachers were employed as detectives to visit the prisoners, engage them in conversation and try to lure them into saying something that could be used as evidence against them.

Source: *Bradford of Plymouth* by William Smith

PEACE

To the right of *Liberty's* pedestal, *Peace* is crowned with a wreath to indicate honor, for "blessed are the peacemakers, for they will be called children of God." (Matthew 5:9) In her left hand, *Peace* holds an olive branch which signifies a spirit of reconciliation. Throughout history, the olive branch has represented peace in Scripture, literature, and culture. Several countries and governmental organizations feature an olive branch in their flags or insignia, including the United States, Italy, Cyprus, and the United Nations.

At her feet, *Peace* stands next to a cornucopia, also called a horn of plenty, which has become symbolic of the traditional American holiday of Thanksgiving. The Pilgrims regularly sought God's will through prayer and fasting at Plymouth Colony. They routinely offered prayers of thanksgiving—acknowledging that "by the good providence and blessing of God, we have enjoyed such plenty as though the windows of heaven had been opened to us. How few, weak, and raw were we at our first beginning... yet God wrought our peace for us."[176]

"Harvest time had now come, and then instead of famine, God gave them plenty, and the face of things was changed, to the rejoicing of the hearts of many for which they blessed God."

- Governor William Bradford

"Is life so dear, or peace so sweet, as to be purchased at the price of chains and slavery? Forbid it, Almighty God! I know not what course others may take, but as for me, give me liberty or give me death!"

- Patrick Henry (1736-1799), Founding Father, orator and first governor of Virginia

TYRANNY

To the left of *Liberty's* pedestal, *Tyranny* is revealed as a defeated foe. With his hand lifted to heaven, the conquering hero stands with his foot on *Tyranny's* neck in the manner of King David who proclaimed, "You armed me with strength for battle; you humbled my adversaries before me. I pursued my enemies and crushed them… they could not rise; they fell beneath my feet." (2 Samuel 22:40, 38-39) In 1593, the Church of England was eager to silence a young influential Welsh Separatist preacher and writer by the name of John Penry. After several early brushes with the law, Penry was eventually arrested for preaching in a Separatist church. While he languished in jail, church officials ransacked his home for evidence of a capital crime that could justify his execution—and found nothing. But as they rifled through Penry's personal papers, they came across an unpublished draft of a petition to the queen. Seizing their opportunity, church officials declared Penry's petition offensive to the crown, and charged him with sedition. He spent just two months in prison. Refusing his desperate pleas to say a final goodbye to his wife and four young daughters—Penry was taken to a public square late one afternoon in London and hanged. Heralded as a martyr after his death, Penry was one of the untold thousands who suffered under England's cruel oppression. For the Pilgrims who came seeking a new life in America, Plymouth Colony represented freedom from such tyranny—and the opportunity to live, worship, and govern themselves according to their God-given freedom.

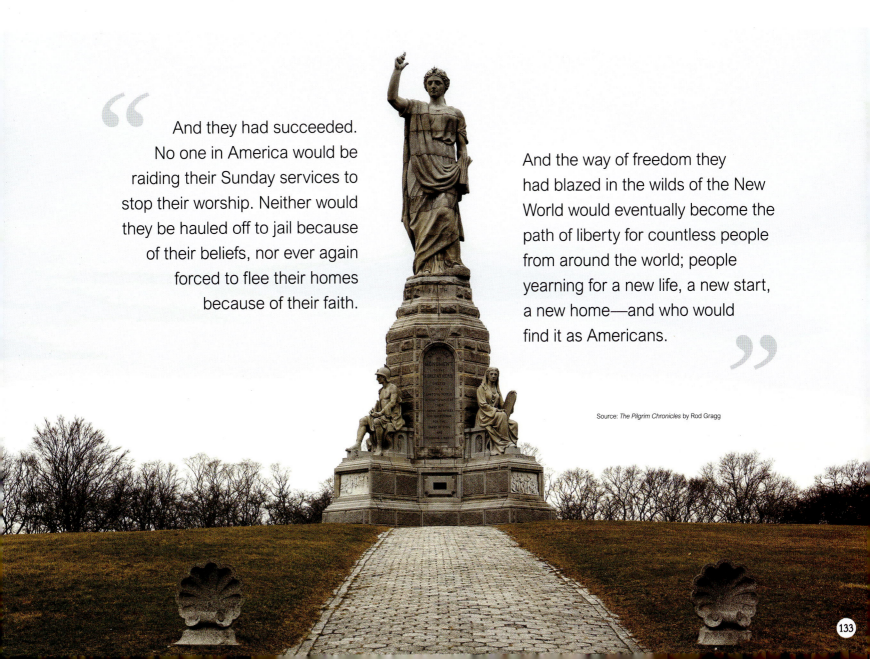

> And they had succeeded. No one in America would be raiding their Sunday services to stop their worship. Neither would they be hauled off to jail because of their beliefs, nor ever again forced to flee their homes because of their faith. And the way of freedom they had blazed in the wilds of the New World would eventually become the path of liberty for countless people from around the world; people yearning for a new life, a new start, a new home—and who would find it as Americans.

Source: *The Pilgrim Chronicles* by Rod Gragg

MONUMENT TO THE FOREFATHERS.—The Pilgrim Society of Plymouth, Mass., have accepted the design of Hammatt Billings, Esq., for a national monument to the forefathers, an effort is making to procure the requisite funds. The monument is to be erected at Plymouth. The structure will be crowned by a colossal figure 70 feet in height; and four others, seated upon the buttresses of the pedestal, will have a height of 38 feet. The panels below the figures are filled with alto-reliefs of "The Departure from Delf- Haven," "The Signing of the Social Compact in the Cabin of the May Flower," "The Landing at Plymouth," and "The First Treaty with the Indians." Upon the four large faces of the main pedestal are large panels, to contain records of the principal events in the history of the Pilgrims, with the names of those who came over in the May Flower. The entire height of the monument will be 150 feet, and it will be 80 feet at the base.

MARBLE BAS-RELIEF PANEL: THE PILGRIM'S LANDING

"We look around us, and behold the hills and promontories where the anxious eyes of our fathers first saw the places of habitation and of rest. We feel the cold which benumbed, and listen to the winds which pierced them. Beneath us is the Rock, on which New England received the feet of the Pilgrims. We seem even to behold them, as they struggle with the elements, and, with toilsome efforts, gain the shore. We listen to the chiefs in council; we see the mild dignity of Carver and of Bradford; the decisive and soldierlike air and manner of Standish; the devout Brewster; the enterprising Allerton; the general firmness and thoughtfulness of the whole band; their conscious joy for dangers escaped; their deep solicitude about danger to come; their trust in Heaven; their high religious faith, full of confidence and anticipation; all of these seem to belong to this place, and to be present upon this occasion, to fill us with reverence and admiration."

Source: Plymouth Oration by Daniel Webster, December 22, 1820

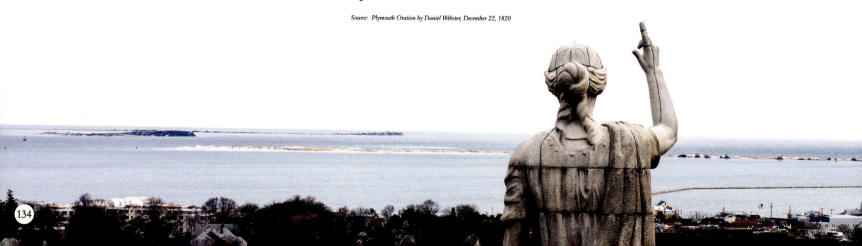

"Here is the nation God has builded by our hands. What shall we do with it?"

- Woodrow Wilson (1856-1924), former Governor of New Jersey, President of Princeton University, and 28th President of the United States

APPENDIX

FOOTNOTES & ENDNOTES:

1. Gragg, Rod. *The Pilgrim Chronicles*. Regnery Publishing, 2014, p.9.
2. Ibid, p.9.
3. Ibid, p.10-11.
4. Ibid, p.14.
5. Ibid, p.27-28.
6. Ibid, p.32.
7. Ibid, p.33.
8. Smith, Bradford. *Bradford Of Plymouth*. 1st ed., Lippincott, 1951, p.48.
9. Bradford, William, and Harold Paget. *Of Plymouth Plantation*. Dover Publications, 2006, p.7.
10. Gragg, Rod. *The Pilgrim Chronicles*. Regnery Publishing, 2014, p.63.
11. Bartlett, Robert Merrill. *The Faith Of The Pilgrims*. United Church Press, 1978, p.18.
12. Bradford, William, and Harold Paget. *Of Plymouth Plantation*. Dover Publications, 2006, p.7.
13. Ibid, p.8.
14. Ibid, p. 8.
15. Ibid, pp. 3-4.
16. Ibid, p. 20.
17. Bradford, William. *Bradford's History Of The Plymouth Settlement, 1608-1650*. E.P. Dutton & Co., 1920, p. 20.
18. Ibid, p. 20.
19. Ibid, p. 33.
20. Gragg, Rod. *The Pilgrim Chronicles*. Regnery Publishing, 2014, p.106.
21. Bradford, William. *Bradford's History Of The Plymouth Settlement, 1608-1650*. E.P. Dutton & Co., 1920, p. 43.
22. Ibid, pp. 37-38.
23. Ibid, pp. 49.
24. Bradford, William. *Bradford's History Of The Plymouth Settlement, 1608-1650*. E.P. Dutton & Co., 1920, pp. 58.
25. Ibid, pp. 58.
26. Bartlett, Robert Merrill. *The Pilgrim Way*. Pilgrim Press, 1971, p. 231.
27. Bradford, William. *Of Plymouth Plantation 1620-1647*. Intr. By Francis Murphy. 1st ed., XXVIII, 1981, p. 67.
28. Bradford, William. *Bradford's History Of The Plymouth Settlement, 1608-1650*. E.P. Dutton & Co., 1920, p. 69.
29. Bradford, William, and Harold Paget. *Of Plymouth Plantation*. Dover Publications, 2006, p. 64.
30. Bradford, William. *Bradford's History Of The Plymouth Settlement, 1608-1650*. E.P. Dutton & Co., 1920, p. 226.
31. Davis, William T. *The Proceedings At The Celebration By The Pilgrim Society, At Plymouth, August 1st, 1889, Of The Completion Of The National Monument To The Pilgrims*. Avery & Doten, 1889, p. 6.
32. Ibid, pp. 6-7.
33. Gomes, Peter J. *The Pilgrim Society, 1820-1970*. The Pilgrim Society, 1971, p. 9.
34. Baker, J., 2020. *Plymouth Rock's Own Story*. Plymouth: The Pilgrim Society, p.12.
35. Ibid, see copyright page description.
36. Davis, William T. *The Proceedings At The Celebration By The Pilgrim Society, At Plymouth, August 1St, 1889, Of The Completion Of The National Monument To The Pilgrims*. Avery & Doten, 1889, p. 10.
37. O'Gorman, James F. *Accomplished In All Departments Of Art, Hammatt Billings Of Boston, 1818-1874*. University Of Massachusetts Press, 1998, p. 226.
38. Ibid, p. 38.
39. Ibid, p. 9.
40. Ibid, p. 153.
41. Stoddard, Richard. "Hammatt Billings, Artist and Architect". *Old-Time New England Magazine*, Vol. LXII, No. 3, Jan-Mar 1972, p. 63.
42. "National Monument To The Forefathers". *The Illustrated Pilgrim Memorial*, 1864, p. 39.
43. O'Gorman, James F. "The Colossus Of Plymouth: Hammatt Billings' National Monument To The Forefathers". *Journal Of The Society Of Architectural Historians*, vol 54, no. 3, 1995, p. 284.
44. Lincoln, Abraham. Abraham Lincoln papers: Series 1. General Correspondence. 1833 to 1916: National Monument to the Forefathers, Monday, Printed Circular. 1861. Manuscript/Mixed Material. Retrieved from the Library of Congress, <www.loc.gov/item/mal0910900/>.
45. "Proclamation 106—Thanksgiving Day, 1863 | The American Presidency Project". *Presidency.Ucsb.Edu*, 2020, https://www.presidency.ucsb.edu/documents/proclamation-106-thanksgiving-day-1863.
46. Gomes, Peter J. *The Pilgrim Society, 1820-1970*. The Pilgrim Society, 1971, p.17.
47. "The Illustrated Pilgrim Memorial". Issued 1864, p. 32, Accessed 21 July 2021.
48. "National Monument To The Forefathers". *The Illustrated Pilgrim Memorial*, 1864, p. 40.
49. The Boston Daily Advertiser, November 16, 1874.
50. Boston Daily Globe, Morning Edition, November 16, 1874.
51. While many respected historians credit Gov. Oliver Ames for sponsoring the cost of Faith, there is evidence to suggest otherwise. Oliver Ames, Jr. (1807-1877) was the uncle of Gov. Oliver Ames (1831-1895), and the similarity of name and close family connection can lead to confusion. Records from the Pilgrim Society credit Hon. Oliver Ames of Easton for underwriting *Faith* and confirm the statue's $32,300 cost "was paid for by the heirs of Mr. Ames, who died before its completion." A second source confirms *Faith* was "underwritten by Honorable Oliver Ames, a Plymouth native then living in Easton," and that "Mr. Ames did not survive to see his donation in place, but his heirs paid the cost of $32,300 for it." To determine which "Oliver" sponsored Faith—Oliver Ames, Jr., the uncle, or his nephew, Oliver Ames, the Governor—the following should be considered. While both men resided in Easton, Massachusetts, only Oliver, Jr. was born in Plymouth before making his home in Easton. Bearing that in mind, only Oliver, Jr. could rightly be termed "a Plymouth native." Each man held public office, so the title "Honorable" is applicable to both. The determining factor is the year of each man's death. Oliver Ames, Jr. died on March 9, 1877, exactly 5 months before the statue of *Faith* was installed on August 9, 1877. By contrast, Gov. Oliver Ames died on October 22, 1895, several years after the Forefathers monument was completed and dedicated in 1889. While both men shared a name, title, and family tree in common—only one died before the statue of *Faith* was installed, requiring his generous donation to be settled by the heirs of his estate. For these reasons, *Faith's* benefactor can rightly be attributed to Hon. Oliver Ames, Jr., the former Massachusetts State Senator, railroad executive and philanthropist, who was born in Plymouth and resided in Easton, Massachusetts, until his death in 1877.
52. "Historic Hallowell - Solid Foundations - Hallowell Granite". *Historichallowell.Mainememory.Net*, 2019, http://historichallowell.mainememory.net/page/1506/display.html. Accessed 6 Aug 2019.
53. Maxwell, Rev. Richard Howland. "Plymouth's Grand Old Lady". *The Mayflower Quarterly*, Vol. 69, No. 2, June 2003, pp. 221.
54. http://mass.gov/dcr/stewardship/rmp/rmp-forefathers.htm
55. Russell, W., 1864. *Pilgrim Memorials, and Guide to Plymouth*. 3rd ed. Boston: Crosby, Nichols and company, p.194.
56. Gragg, Rod. *The Pilgrim Chronicles*. Regnery Publishing, 2014, pp. 33.
57. Bradford, William. *The History Of Plymouth Colony*. Pub. For The Classics Club By W.J. Black, 1948, p.10.
58. Robinson, John. *The Works Of John Robinson, Pastor Of The Pilgrim Fathers, Volume 3*. John Snow, 1851, p. 155.
59. Bradford, William. *Bradford's History Of The Plymouth Settlement, 1608-1650*. E.P. Dutton & Co., 1920, p. 9.

FOOTNOTES & ENDNOTES:

60. Bradford, William. *The History Of Plymouth Colony*. Pub. For The Classics Club By W.J. Black, 1948, p.6.
61. Bradford, William. *Bradford's History Of The Plymouth Settlement, 1608-1650*. E.P. Dutton & Co., 1920, p. 15.
62. Ibid, p. 9.
63. Ibid, p. 15.
64. Bradford, William. *The History Of Plymouth Colony*. Pub. For The Classics Club By W.J. Black, 1948, p.30.
65. Bradford, William. *Bradford's History Of The Plymouth Settlement, 1608-1650*. E.P. Dutton & Co., 1920, p. 77.
66. Ibid, p. 83.
67. Gragg, Rod. *The Pilgrim Chronicles*. Regnery Publishing, 2014, pp. 259-260.
68. Bradford, William. *Bradford's History Of The Plymouth Settlement, 1608-1650*. E.P. Dutton & Co., 1920, p. 49.
69. Robinson, John. *The Works Of John Robinson, Pastor Of The Pilgrim Fathers, Volume 3*. John Snow, 1851, p. 70.
70. Gragg, Rod. *The Pilgrim Chronicles*. Regnery Publishing, 2014, p. 8.
71. Bradford, William. *The History Of Plymouth Colony*. Pub. For The Classics Club By W.J. Black, 1948, p. 32.
72. Milbrandt, Jay. *They Came For Freedom: The Forgotten, Epic Adventure Of The Pilgrims*. Nelson Books, 2017, p. 123.
73. Paget, Harold. *Bradford's History Of The Plymouth Settlement*. E.P. Dutton & Company, 1920, p. 64.
74. Ibid, p. 69.
75. Ibid, p. 79.
76. Ibid, p. 80.
77. Doherty, Kieran. *William Bradford*. Twenty-First Century Books, 1999, p. 109.
78. Paget, Harold. *Bradford's History Of The Plymouth Settlement*. E.P. Dutton & Company, 1920, p. 66.
79. "Founders Online: From John Adams To Massachusetts Militia, 11 October 1798". Founders.Archives.Gov, 2020, https://founders.archives.gov/documents/Adams/99-02-02-3102.
80. Paget, Harold. *Bradford's History Of The Plymouth Settlement*. E.P. Dutton & Company, 1920, p. 15.
81. Paget, Harold. *Bradford's History Of The Plymouth Settlement*. E.P. Dutton & Company, 1920, p. 17.
82. Robinson, John. *The Works Of John Robinson, Pastor Of The Pilgrim Fathers, Vol. I*. Reed And Pardon, 1851, p. 34.
83. Kamrath, Angela E. *The Miracle Of America*. 2nd ed., Xulon, 2015, p. 187.
84. Bartlett, Robert Merrill. *The Faith Of The Pilgrims*. United Church Press, 1978, p. 53.
85. Bradford, William. *Bradford's History Of The Plymouth Settlement, 1608-1650*. E.P. Dutton & Co., 1920, pp. 60-61.
86. "Priesthood Of All Believers | Christianity". *Encyclopedia Britannica*, 2020, https://www.britannica.com/topic/priesthood-of-all-believers. Accessed 19 Aug 2020.
87. Paget, Harold. *Bradford's History Of The Plymouth Settlement*. E.P. Dutton & Company, 1920, p. 21.
88. Medved, Michael. *The American Miracle*. 1st ed., Crown Forum, 2016, p. 46.
89. Bradford, William. *The History Of Plymouth Colony*. Pub. For The Classics Club By W.J. Black, 1948, p. 66.
90. Bradford, William. *The History Of Plymouth Colony*. W.J. Black, 1948, p.123.
91. Bradford, William, and Harold Paget. *Of Plymouth Plantation*. Dover Publications, 2006, p. 50.
92. Bradford, William. *The History Of Plymouth Colony*. Pub. For The Classics Club By W.J. Black, 1948, p. 30.
93. Paget, Harold. *Bradford's History Of The Plymouth Settlement*. E.P. Dutton & Company, 1920, p.75.
94. Bradford, William. *Bradford's History Of The Plymouth Settlement, 1608-1650*. E.P. Dutton & Co., 1920, p. 7.
95. Ibid, p. 28.
96. Haskins, George L. "The Legal Heritage Of Plymouth Colony". *University Of Pennsylvania Law Review*, vol 110, no. 6, 1962, p. 847. JSTOR, doi:10.2307/3310640.
97. Bradford, William. *Bradford's History Of The Plymouth Settlement, 1608-1650*. E.P. Dutton & Co., 1920, p. 76.
98. Milbrandt, Jay. *They Came For Freedom: The Forgotten, Epic Adventure Of The Pilgrims*. Nelson Books, 2017, p.130.
99. Quincy Adams, John. "*An Oration, Delivered At Plymouth, December 22, 1802. At The Anniversary Commemoration Of The First Landing Of Our Ancestors, At That Place*". 1802.
100. Bradford, William. *Bradford's History Of The Plymouth Settlement, 1608-1650*. E.P. Dutton & Co., 1920, p. 76.
101. Ibid, p. 55-56.
102. Smith, Bradford. *Bradford Of Plymouth*. 1st ed., Lippincott, 1951, p. 33.
103. Stratton, Eugene Aubrey. *Plymouth Colony, Its History & People, 1620-1691*. 1st ed., Ancestry Pub., 1986, p. 156.
104. Ibid, p. 157.
105. Haskins, George L. "The Legal Heritage Of Plymouth Colony". *University Of Pennsylvania Law Review*, vol 110, no. 6, 1962, p. 848-849. JSTOR, doi:10.2307/3310640.
106. Lutz, Donald S. *Colonial Origins Of The American Constitution: A Documentary History*. Liberty Fund, Inc., 1998, p. 61.
107. Haskins, George L. "The Legal Heritage Of Plymouth Colony". *University Of Pennsylvania Law Review*, vol 110, no. 6, 1962, p. 851. JSTOR, doi:10.2307/3310640.
108. Powers, Edwin. *Crime And Punishment In Early Massachusetts, 1620-1692,*. Beacon Press, 1966, p. 28.
109. Bartlett, Robert Merrill. *The Faith Of The Pilgrims*. United Church Press, 1978, p. 117.
110. Powers, Edwin. *Crime And Punishment In Early Massachusetts, 1620-1692,*. Beacon Press, 1966, p. 96.
111. Haskins, George L. "The Legal Heritage Of Plymouth Colony". *University Of Pennsylvania Law Review*, vol 110, no. 6, 1962, p. 849. JSTOR, doi:10.2307/3310640.
112. Ibid, p. 855. JSTOR, doi:10.2307/3310640.
113. Willison, George F. *Saints & Strangers*. Parnassus Imprints, 1945, p.166.
114. Bradford, William. *The History Of Plymouth Colony*. W.J. Black, 1948, p.102.
115. Ibid, p.104.
116. Bradford, William. *Bradford's History Of The Plymouth Settlement, 1608-1650*. E.P. Dutton & Co., 1920, p. 293.
117. Bradford, William. *The History Of Plymouth Colony*. W.J. Black, 1948, p.363.
118. Bradford, William. *Bradford's History Of The Plymouth Settlement, 1608-1650*. E.P. Dutton & Co., 1920, p. 294.
119. Bradford, William. *The History Of Plymouth Colony*. W.J. Black, 1948, p.364
120. Ibid, p.106.
121. Gragg, Rod. *The Pilgrim Chronicles*. Regnery History, 2014, p. 252.
122. Ibid, p.54.
123. Ibid, p.54.
124. Ibid, p.54.
125. Ibid, p.55.
126. Ibid, p.55.
127. Ibid, p.58.
128. Cremin, Lawrence A. *American Education: The Colonial Experience, 1607-1783*. Harper Torchbooks, 1970, p. 41.
129. Bartlett, Robert Merrill. *The Faith Of The Pilgrims*. United Church Press, 1978, pp.43.

FOOTNOTES & ENDNOTES:

130. Bartlett, Robert Merrill. *The Faith Of The Pilgrims*. United Church Press, 1978, p.45.
131. Bradford, William. *The History Of Plymouth Colony*. W.J. Black, 1948, p.110.
132. Bartlett, Robert Merrill. *The Faith Of The Pilgrims*. United Church Press, 1978, p.44.
133. "Education In Colonial America | Robert A. Peterson". *Fee.Org*, 2020, https://fee.org/article/education-in-colonial-america/.
134. Cremin, Lawrence A. *American Education: The Colonial Experience, 1607-1783*. Harper Torchbooks, 1970, p.51.
135. Cremin, Lawrence A. *American Education: The Colonial Experience, 1607-1783*. Harper Torchbooks, 1970, p. 40.
136. "Education In Colonial America | Robert A. Peterson". *Fee.Org*, 2020, https://fee.org/articles/education-in-colonial-america/.
137. Ibid.
138. Newcombe, Jerry. *The Book That Made America*. Nordskog Pub., Inc., 2009, p. 105.
139. Bradford, William. *Bradford's History Of The Plymouth Settlement, 1608-1650*. E.P. Dutton & Co., 1920, p. 55.
140. Bradford, William. *The History Of Plymouth Colony*. W.J. Black, 1948, p.72.
141. Bradford, William, and Harold Paget. *Of Plymouth Plantation*. Dover Publications, 2006, p.55.
142. Bartlett, Robert Merrill. *The Faith Of The Pilgrims*. United Church Press, 1978, pp. 155-156.
143. Ibid, p. 156.
144. Bradford, William. *The History Of Plymouth Colony*. W.J. Black, 1948, p. xxi.
145. Bartlett, Robert Merrill. *The Faith Of The Pilgrims*. United Church Press, 1978, p. 158.
146. Ibid, p. 158.
147. Smith, Bradford. *Bradford Of Plymouth*. 1st ed., Lippincott, 1951, p. 320.
148. Ibid, p. 320.
149. Ibid, p. 319.
150. Bradford, William. *Of Plymouth Plantation 1620-1647*. Intr. By Francis Murphy. 1st ed., XXVIII, 1981, p.vii.
151. Smith, Bradford. *Bradford Of Plymouth*. 1st ed., Lippincott, 1951, p. 320.
152. Gragg, Rod. *The Pilgrim Chronicles*. Regnery Publishing, 2014, p.93.
153. Bartlett, Robert Merrill. *The Faith Of The Pilgrims*. United Church Press, 1978, p. 99.
154. Ibid, p. 89.
155. Ibid, p. 169.
156. Ibid, p. 125.
157. Griffis, William Elliot. "What the Pilgrim Fathers Accomplished." *The North American Review*, vol. 213, no. 782, 1921, pp. 44–51. *JSTOR*, www.jstor.org/stable/25120655. Accessed 9 Mar. 2020.
158. Bartlett, Robert Merrill. *The Faith Of The Pilgrims*. United Church Press, 1978, p. 124.
159. Gragg, Rod. *The Pilgrim Chronicles*. Regnery Publishing, 2014, p.88.
160. Bradford, William, and Harold Paget. *Of Plymouth Plantation*. Dover Publications, 2006, p.21.
161. Bradford, William. *Bradford's History Of The Plymouth Settlement, 1608-1650*. E.P. Dutton & Co., 1920, p.203.
162. Bartlett, Robert Merrill. *The Faith Of The Pilgrims*. United Church Press, 1978, p.171.
163. Ibid, p.149.
164. Bradford, William. *Bradford's History Of The Plymouth Settlement, 1608-1650*. E.P. Dutton & Co., 1920, p. 116.
165. Ibid, p. 116.
166. Ibid, p. 115.
167. Smith, Bradford. *Bradford Of Plymouth*. 1st ed., Lippincott, 1951, p.20-21.
168. Ibid, p.154.
169. Webster, Noah. *History Of The United States: To Which Is Prefixed A Brief Historical Account Of Our English Ancestors ... And Of The Conquest Of South America By The Spaniards*. Durrie & Peck, 1832, p. 301.
170. https://www.archives.gov/founding-docs/declaration-transcript
171. Bradford, William, and Harold Paget. *Of Plymouth Plantation*. Dover Publications, 2006, p.226.
172. Gragg, Rod. *The Pilgrim Chronicles*. Regnery Publishing, 2014, p.261.
173. Bradford, William, and Harold Paget. *Of Plymouth Plantation*. Dover Publications, 2006, p. 54.
174. Smith, Bradford. *Bradford Of Plymouth*. 1st ed., Lippincott, 1951, p. 61-62.
175. Ibid, p. 32.
176. Young, Alexander. *Chronicles Of The Pilgrim Fathers Of The Colony Of Plymouth, From 1602 To 1625*. 2nd ed., C.C. Little And J. Brown, 1844, p. 355.

PHOTOGRAPHY CREDITS

1 – Cover image courtesy of Hawk Visuals. www.hawkvisualsmedia.com

8, 9 – Drone photography courtesy of Sojourner Media. www.sojourner-media.com

10, 11 – Drone photography courtesy of Sojourner Media. www.sojourner-media.com

15 – *All Saints' Church in Babworth* and *Pilgrims' Way Footpath* courtesy of Wrestling and Belinda Brewster.

16 – *Entrance to Manor Grounds* courtesy of Bassetlaw Museum in Nottinghamshire, England. (Bassetlaw Museum, Amcott House, 40 Grove Street, Retford, Nottinghamshire, DN22 6LD) To schedule a tour or learn more, visit: www.bassetlawmuseum.org.uk and www.pilgrimroots.co.uk

16 – *Farmhouse of Scrooby Manor* courtesy of Wrestling and Belinda Brewster.

21 – *Mayflower* graphic courtesy of Jeff Goertzen, Southern California Newsgroup.

22 – Images courtesy of Sojourner Media. www.sojourner-media.com

24 – *Hammatt Billings* and *Pharoah's Court* courtesy of Wellesley College Library, Special Collections. Special thanks to Professor Emeritus James F. O'Gorman and Associate Curator Mariana S. Oller for their invaluable assistance.

26 – *Pilgrim Society Membership Certificate* courtesy of courtesy of Wellesley College Library, Special Collections. Special thanks to Professor Emeritus James F. O'Gorman and Associate Curator Mariana S. Oller for their invaluable assistance.

30 – *Granite Shell* courtesy of Sojourner Media. www.sojourner-media.com

32 – TOP LEFT: *Sands Quarry* courtesy of the Vinalhaven Historical Society.

32 – TOP RIGHT: *Bodwell Cutting Shed* courtesy of Penobscot Marine Museum.

32 – BOTTOM LEFT: *Hallowell Granite Quarry* courtesy of Penobscot Marine Museum.

33 – TOP RIGHT, LEFT: *Stonecutters in Work Sheds* courtesy of Maine Historic Preservation Commission.

33 – BOTTOM: *Outdoor Carvers by Rail Tracks* courtesy of Penobscot Marine Museum.

34 – *Faith Under Construction* courtesy of Maine Historic Preservation Commission.

35 – TOP RIGHT: *Faith in Cutting Yard* courtesy of Maine Historic Preservation Commission.

36 – LEFT: *Harper's Weekly* courtesy of HathiTrust.

39 – BOTTOM: Images of medals courtesy of Coin & Currency Institute, Williston, Vermont.

42 – Images courtesy of Sojourner Media. www.sojourner-media.com

44, 45 – Drone photography courtesy of Sojourner Media. www.sojourner-media.com

46, 47 – Images courtesy of Sojourner Media. www.sojourner-media.com

48, 49 – Drone photography courtesy of Sojourner Media. www.sojourner-media.com

50 – Image courtesy of Sojourner Media. www.sojourner-media.com

51, 54, 55, 56 – Drone photography courtesy of Sojourner Media. www.sojourner-media.com

57 – All images courtesy of Bassetlaw Museum in Nottinghamshire, England. (Bassetlaw Museum, Amcott House, 40 Grove Street, Retford, Nottinghamshire, DN22 6LD) To learn more, visit: www.bassetlawmuseum.org.uk and www.pilgrimroots.co.uk

58 – *View from National Monument to Standish* courtesy of Emerson Collection/Longmeadow Historical Society.

59 – Drone photography courtesy of Sojourner Media. www.sojourner-media.com

60 – TOP RIGHT: *The Seas Were So High* courtesy of Mike Haywood Art. www.mikehaywoodart.uk

60, 61 – Drone photography courtesy of Sojourner Media. www.sojourner-media.com

63, 64, 65, 66 – Images courtesy of Sojourner Media. www.sojourner-media.com

67 – Inset image of *Priestly Garment* courtesy of Sojourner Media. www.sojourner-media.com

68, 69, 70 – Images courtesy of Sojourner Media. www.sojourner-media.com

71 – TOP LEFT: *Morality Awaits Delivery* courtesy of Maine Historic Preservation Commission.

71 – BOTTOM RIGHT: *Forefathers Monument* courtesy of Debra Riservato.

72 – Images courtesy of Sojourner Media. www.sojourner-media.com

74, 75 – *Mayflower Passengers* graphic courtesy of Pilgrim Hall Museum, Plymouth, Massachusetts. www.pilgrimhall.org

76, 77, 79, 82 – Images courtesy of Sojourner Media. www.sojourner-media.com

85 – *Historic Leyden Street* courtesy of Wayne Collamore. www.WayneCollamorePhotography.com

88 – Images of *Law* and *Mercy* courtesy of Ben Eaton Creative. www.beneatoncreative.com

89 – *Mayflower Docked at Plymouth* courtesy of Wayne Collamore. www.WayneCollamorePhotography.com

PHOTOGRAPHY CREDITS

90 – Images courtesy of Sojourner Media. www.sojourner-media.com

91 – *Forefathers Monument at Night* courtesy of Christopher Setterlund. www.ChristopherSetterlund.com

92 – Images courtesy of Sojourner Media. www.sojourner-media.com

93 – LEFT: *Statue of Massasoit* courtesy of Sojourner Media. www.sojourner-media.com

93 – CENTER: *Massasoit at Sunrise* courtesy of Mark Foley.

93 – BOTTOM: *Plymouth Rock Canopy at Night* courtesy of Wayne Collamore. www.WayneCollamorePhotography.com

94 – Drone photography courtesy of Sojourner Media. www.sojourner-media.com

96, 97, 100 – Images courtesy of Sojourner Media. www.sojourner-media.com

101 – *Forefathers Monument* courtesy of Debra Riservato.

102, 104, 106, 108, 109, 110, 111, 112 – Images courtesy of Sojourner Media. www.sojourner-media.com

114 – *Forefathers Monument Under the Milky Way* courtesy of Richard Noyes Photography. www.richardjnoyes.com

116, 117 – Images courtesy of Sojourner Media. www.sojourner-media.com

118 – *Pathway to the Forefathers Monument* courtesy of Debra Riservato.

119 – *Faith and Liberty* courtesy of Debra Riservato.

120 – TOP: *Replica of the 1627 Aptucxet Trading Post at the Aptucxet Trading Post Museum*, by permission of the Creative Commons Attribution-Share Alike 4.0 International license. Author: Vejlenser, Dated: 12 July 2017. https://commons.wikimedia.org/wiki/File:Aptucxet_Trading_Post_1.jpg

121 – TOP LEFT: *Aerial View of the Forefathers Monument* courtesy of Blaine Kitchen, taken 2000 feet above ground in a Cessna 172.

121 – BOTTOM: Drone photography courtesy of Sojourner Media. www.sojourner-media.com

122 – *Pilgrim Overboard* courtesy of Mike Haywood Art. Mike Haywood Art. www.mikehaywoodart.uk

124 – Image courtesy of Sojourner Media. www.sojourner-media.com

125 – *Forefathers Monument* courtesy of Richard Noyes Photography. www.richardjnoyes.com

126, 127, 128, 129, 130, 131, 132, 133, 134 – Drone photography courtesy of Sojourner Media. www.sojourner-media.com

135 – *Looking Up At the Forefathers Monument* courtesy of Debra Riservato.

BIBLIOGRAPHY

Baker, James W. *Plymouth Rock's Own Story*. The Pilgrim Society, 2020

Bartlett, Robert Merrill. *The Faith Of The Pilgrims*. United Church Press, 1978

Bartlett, Robert Merrill. *The Pilgrim Way*. Pilgrim Press, 1971

Bradford, William, and Harold Paget. *Of Plymouth Plantation*. Dover Publications, 2006

Bradford, William. *Bradford's History Of The Plymouth Settlement, 1608-1650*. E.P. Dutton & Co., 1920

Bradford, William. *The History Of Plymouth Colony*. W.J. Black, 1948

Bradford, William. *Of Plymouth Plantation 1620-1647*. Intr. By Francis Murphy, 1981

Cremin, Lawrence A. *American Education: The Colonial Experience, 1607-1783*. Harper Torchbooks, 1970

Doherty, Kieran. *William Bradford*. Twenty-First Century Books, 1999

Gomes, Peter J. *The Pilgrim Society, 1820-1970*. The Pilgrim Society, 1971

Gragg, Rod. *The Pilgrim Chronicles*. Regnery Publishing, 2014

Griffis, William Elliot. *What the Pilgrim Fathers Accomplished*. The North American Review, 1921

Haskins, George L. *The Legal Heritage Of Plymouth Colony*. University Of Pennsylvania Law Review, 1962

Kamrath, Angela E. *The Miracle Of America*. Xulon, 2015

Lutz, Donald S. *Colonial Origins Of The American Constitution: A Documentary History*. Liberty Fund, Inc., 1998

Medved, Michael. *The American Miracle*. Crown Forum, 2016

Milbrandt, Jay. *They Came For Freedom: The Forgotten, Epic Adventure Of The Pilgrims*. Nelson Books, 2017

Newcombe, Jerry. *The Book That Made America*. Nordskog Pub., Inc., 2009

O'Gorman, James F. *Accomplished In All Departments Of Art, Hammatt Billings Of Boston, 1818-1874*. University Of Massachusetts Press, 1998

Paget, Harold. *Bradford's History Of The Plymouth Settlement*. E.P. Dutton & Company, 1920

Powers, Edwin. *Crime And Punishment In Early Massachusetts, 1620-1692*. Beacon Press, 1966

Robinson, John. *The Works Of John Robinson, Pastor Of The Pilgrim Fathers, Vol. I*. Reed And Pardon, 1851

Robinson, John. *The Works Of John Robinson, Pastor Of The Pilgrim Fathers, Vol. 3*. John Snow, 1851

Russell, William S., *Pilgrim Memorials, and Guide to Plymouth*. Boston: Crosby, Nichols and Company, 1864

Smith, Bradford. *Bradford Of Plymouth*. Lippincott, 1951

Stratton, Eugene Aubrey. *Plymouth Colony, Its History & People, 1620-1691*. Ancestry Pub., 1986

Webster, Noah. *History Of The United States: To Which Is Prefixed A Brief Historical Account Of Our English Ancestors ... And Of The Conquest Of South America By The Spaniards*. Durrie & Peck, 1832

Willison, George F. *Saints & Strangers*. Parnassus Imprints, 1945

Young, Alexander. *Chronicles Of The Pilgrim Fathers Of The Colony Of Plymouth, From 1602 to 1625*. C.C. Little and J. Brown, 1844